NFL

Football

Published in the United States
by Triumph Books,
644 South Clark Street,
Chicago, Illinois 60605,
in association with Carlton Books Limited, 1996

Printed and bound in Italy

ISBN 1-57243-155-5

This book is available in quantity at special discounts for your group or
organization. For further information, contact:
Triumph Books
644 South Clark Street
Chicago, Illinios 60605
(312) 939-3330
Fax (312) 663-3557

**The publishers would like to thank NFL Photos for their kind
permission to reproduce many of the pictures in this book.
Photographer credits are as follows:** John E. Biever: 89, 91, 95, 120 right
middle; Vernon Biever: 19, 50 left; David Boss: 16-17 top, 106-7, 109, 120 bottom
middle, 122; Peter Brouillet: 58, 61; Greg Crisp: 26, 45; Bill Cummings: 98; Scott
Cunningham: 30, 103, 107 right; Gioc Del Pallone: 9 left; Bruce Dierdorff: 41; Brian
Drake: 56; Gin Ellis: 57; Malcolm W. Emmons: 13, 16 left, 81, 87; Mike Fabus: 37;
Nate Fine: 82, 88; James F. Flores: 76, 120 top left; Gerald Gallegos: 52, 67; Pete J.
Groh: 32; Andy Hayt: 40; Jon Hayt: 43; Hall Of Fame: 10 top, 11 top and right mid,
119; Paul Jasienski: 3, 33, 34, 63, 75 left, 96, 102; Allen Kee: 22, 44, 73; Heinz
Kluetmeier: 85; LC Lambrecht: 28, 65, 112, 113 right, 117; Ross Lewis: 14 left;
Long Photography: 97; Richard Mackson: 99; Tak Makita: 83; John McDonough:
53, 70, 92, 94; Al Messerschmidt: 6, 27, 29, 110, 114 top right; Peter Read Miller:
54, 60, 72; Steven Murphy: 59; Patrick Murphy-Racey: 114 bottom left; NFL Photos:
8, 9 top right, 10 bottom right, 11 bottom, 75 right, 77, 82; Darryl Norenberg: 74, 78;
Bernardo Nuñez: 35; Joe Patronite: 42; Al Pereira: 113 left; Richard Raphael: 55, 80;
John H. Reid: 115; Frank Rippon: 12; Bob Rosato: 46, 49, 62, 66, 69; Manny Rubio:
90; Mark Sherengo: 36, 47; Carl Skalak Jr: 50 right, 123; Chuck Solomon: 21; Paul
Spinell: 20, 25, 48, 64, 101, 118-9; Brian Spurlock: 39; Allan Dean Steele: 38, 71;
David Stluka: 24; Kevin Terrell: 105; Tony Tomsic: 14-15 top, 51, 79, 84, 86, 93,
121; Corky Trewin: 108; Greg Trott: 31; Jim Turner: 23, 104; Ron Vesely: 68;
Michael Zagaris: 4–5, 100; Joel Zwink: 33

NFL Football
THE OFFICIAL FANS' GUIDE

TRIUMPH
BOOKS
CHICAGO

Ron Smith

Contents

Introduction......................................6

In The Beginning
The History.......................................8

Everybody Wants to Play for a Winner
The Teams.......................................18

NFL Fans Reach for the Stars
The Stars...50

A Super Way to End Every Season
The Super Bowls.............................74

Fun in the Sun
The Pro Bowl.................................106

Picking and Hoping
The Draft..112

Where Legends Live Forever
NFL Hall of Fame...........................118

Glossary...126

Index...127

No bricks: As a child Jerry Rice used to catch bricks while working with his father. Now he's caught more passes than any receiver in NFL history.

Introduction

The images remain firmly implanted in the mind: Johnny Unitas leading his Baltimore Colts on a desperation drive. Steve Myhra kicking the game-tying field goal with seven seconds remaining. Alan Ameche slamming over the middle for a touchdown, ending the first sudden-death overtime in National Football League Championship Game history.

December 28, 1958. A monumental forward step in league history, viewed by 64,185 fans at New York's Yankee Stadium and millions more across the country on television. The game that lifted the national consciousness of professional football and blazed the trail that would lead to unfathomable popularity, international awareness and untold riches, both in athletic accomplishments and monetary rewards.

Every long journey requires a first step, and this was more like a giant leap for the sport that had not been able to find its way out of the shadows for almost forty years.

Now, nearly four decades later, the NFL's showcase event, the Super Bowl, is viewed from Afghanistan to Zimbabwe and preseason games are being played before sellout crowds on foreign soil. Fall and winter Sunday afternoons and nights and Monday nights belong to the NFL, which beams its highlights into more than 171 countries and territories around the world. The NFL's players have become international personalities and even its April draft, the sometimes-plodding selection process to restock rosters with fresh college talent, is analyzed and dissected for the better part of two days by television cameras and hungry audiences.

Professional football's meteoric rise has been fueled by its own ever-advancing marketing abilities. From the dawning of the television era and the arrival of marketing genius Pete Rozelle in 1960 as its sixth commissioner or President, the NFL has steadily moved to the head of the team sports class. All the polls hail football as America's new National Pastime and such talk is supported by unprecedented attendance figures and the sport's impact on the American public, both at the professional and collegiate levels.

But no amount of marketing will change one basic fact: a sport is only as strong as the product it puts on the field. And professional football has been blessed by a steady stream of gifted athletes whose ever-advancing skills mirror the evolution of its ever-advancing offensive and defensive philosophies.

In the great tradition of modern trend setters Unitas and Jim Brown, such talents as Bart Starr, Larry Csonka, Terry Bradshaw, Walter Payton, Roger Staubach, Lawrence Taylor, Mike Singletary and Joe Montana helped carry the game to new heights of popularity. Coaches like Vince Lombardi, Tom Landry, Chuck Noll, Don Shula, Bill Walsh, Joe Gibbs and Mike Ditka molded sophisticated game plans that created such championship teams as the Packers, Cowboys, Steelers, Dolphins, 49ers, Redskins and Bears.

And the beat goes on. As the NFL barrels toward a new century, such veteran stars as Dan Marino, John Elway, Steve Young, Jerry Rice, and Reggie White are passing the baton to such young lions as Barry Sanders, Junior Seau, Drew Bledsoe, Brett Favre, Emmitt Smith, Marshall Faulk, and Errict Rhett.

The journey continues.

In the Beginning

THE HISTORY OF THE NFL

Papa Bear: George Halas was a long-time player, coach and owner of a Chicago Bears franchise that started as the Decatur Staleys.

I t started inauspiciously at a Canton, Ohio, Hupmobile car dealership when a handful of men, representing ten teams, sowed the seeds that would germinate into a multi-billion dollar bonanza known today as the National Football League. That September 17, 1920, gathering poured the foundation for a professional game that would evolve over the next three-quarters of a century from the single-wing, cloud-of-dust mentality of yesteryear into the sophisticated, one-back, aerial wizardry of the 1990s.

For a mere $100 entry fee that was never collected, ten owners were granted charter franchises in the American Professional Football Association, a union that was cemented with the election of aging all-sports star Jim Thorpe as the league's first president—not because of his administrative acumen, but because of his ability to play football and garner publicity. The APFA would need all of that it could get.

And it would need visionary officials, tough-minded owners and star-quality players who could bring skeptical fans through the turnstiles.

One such visionary was George Halas, a former University of Illinois end who was present at the September meeting as a representative of the Decatur (Ill) Staleys. What brought Halas and his fellow organizers to Ralph Hay's Canton Hupmobile dealership was the fly-by-night status of their professional sport, which was operating primarily in the Midwest in chaotic obscurity.

Professional football was not a new phenomenon. Players had been paid for their abilities as early as the 1890s and athletic clubs had fielded teams on a regional basis for the first two decades of the century. But teams were without structure, player raids were common, collegians were being enticed to play under assumed names and salaries were rising to unmanageable levels. Teams operated independently, without the common-interest restrictions of a league unit. The APFA was an attempt to address those problems.

GROWING PAINS

The 14 teams (four were added during the season) that concluded the 1920 campaign under the APFA umbrella didn't act much differently than those that had competed in 1919. Schedules were self-generated and uneven, owners ignored pledges not to raid opposing rosters and salaries continued to rise. The league, with teams representing five states, did not even keep standings and selected the unbeaten Akron Pros as its first champion by consensus vote.

In 1921, the APFA elected a new president, Joe Carr, and operated under a constitution that restricted player movement and provided needed structure. In 1922, the league played its first season as the NFL and Halas' now Chicago-based team played its first as the Bears. But stability would not come easily. The NFL ranged from ten to 22 teams during the 1920s as poorly financed owners battled for fan support as well as victories. Professional football lagged well behind baseball, college football and boxing as the choice of sports-viewing America.

The league's first breakthrough occurred in 1925, when Halas signed Harold (Red) Grange, the "Galloping Ghost" who had drawn national acclaim for his ball-carrying feats at the University of Illinois. The flamboyant Grange, equal in stature to baseball player Babe Ruth and boxer Jack Dempsey, joined the Bears late in the season and a league-record crowd of 36,000 turned out for his Thanksgiving Day debut—a scoreless tie against the cross-town Cardinals.

But that turnout was dwarfed by the 73,000 fans who paid to see Grange and the Bears meet the Giants in a postseason exhibition game at New York's Polo Grounds and the 75,000 who watched the Bears defeat the semi-pro Los Angeles Tigers a few weeks later at the L.A Coliseum. The NFL had its first superstar and plenty more would

Indian runner: Jim Thorpe, who was voted America's top athlete of the first half of the twentieth century, was the first president of the fledgling NFL.

 Galloping Ghost: When Harold (Red) Grange joined the Chicago Bears, coach George Halas arranged a barnstorming tour to show off his latest signing.

follow. Fullback Ernie Nevers arrived a year after Grange and halfback Johnny (Blood) McNally led a 1929 Green Bay Packers charge that resulted in their first of three consecutive championships. The Bears' 1930 signing of bruising fullback/tackle Bronko Nagurski signaled a new era of power football in Chicago.

A MODERN LOOK

Not even the drawing power of Grange, Nevers, Blood and Nagurski could get the NFL through the Great Depression unscathed. But the economic turmoil that gripped America during the early 1930s had several positive side-effects.

Small-market owners, already strapped to pay the bills, found they could not compete and folded their franchises. By 1931, the NFL was a more-manageable ten-team circuit. By 1932, the number was eight—the lowest membership in league history. But all the teams, with the exception of Green Bay and Portsmouth, were located in major cities and supported by a solid fan base.

The trimmed-down NFL took several giant steps toward prosperity in 1933. Recognizing the need to establish its own personality and break from the mold of the more-conservative college game, officials pushed through innovative measures that would change the course of professional football.

Several were the result of a season-ending 1932 playoff game,

Pioneer: Ernie Nevers was an early NFL fullback. He played only five seasons for the Duluth Eskimos and Cardinals when they were still located in Chicago.

Unstoppable force: Bronko Nagurski was a powerful runner and blocker for the Chicago Bears. He helped the Bears win three NFL titles.

necessitated by a regular-season tie between the Bears and Portsmouth Spartans. The game was scheduled for Chicago's Wrigley Field. But a monster snowstorm buried the city and Halas, in desperation, moved the game to Chicago Stadium—an indoor arena that allowed room for an 80-yard field only. To compensate, the goal posts were moved from the end lines to the goal lines and hashmarks were drawn for ball placement ten yards from the side walls that butted the field. The Bears won the bizarre game, 9-0.

But the significance of that game lives on. The hashmarks and re-positioned goal posts became permanent changes for 1933, as did a rule allowing quarterbacks to pass from any point behind the line of scrimmage. (Previously, they had to be more than five yards behind the line.). The eventual result was a wide-open game utilizing the full field. The NFL also was divided into two divisions, with winners to meet in an annual championship game.

But the 1933 epiphany did not end there. The NFL beefed up its membership to ten teams and introduced three forceful personalities who would play major roles in the game's sometimes-painful, always-colorful evolution. Art Rooney (Pittsburgh Pirates) and Bert Bell (Philadelphia Eagles) entered the league with new teams. Charles Bidwill purchased the Chicago Cardinals. That trio locked arms with holdovers Halas, Curly Lambeau (Packers), Tim Mara (Giants), George Preston Marshall (Redskins) and Carr to form a leadership block that would rule the game for decades.

Ringing the changes: Bert Bell, founder of the Philadelphia Eagles, was the NFL Commissioner from 1946 until his death in 1959.

 Record breaker: Sid Luckman holds the Bears' records for touchdown passes in a game, season and career. Seven in a game is an NFL record.

Court justice, won the 1938 rushing title playing for Pittsburgh. And Mel Hein dominated both sides of the line as a center and linebacker with the New York Giants.

DRAFTING A FUTURE

As the modernized NFL escaped the clutches of economic catastrophe in the mid-1930s, it became clear that the balance of power rested in four cities. The Bears, Packers, Redskins and Giants would combine to win all but one championship from 1933-44.

The have-nots, unable to outbid their powerful opponents for talent, needed a competitive boost. They got it when the NFL voted in 1935 to adopt Bell's proposal for a draft of college players, with teams making selections in inverse order of finish from the previous season. Appropriately, Bell's Eagles were awarded the first pick of the inaugural 1936 draft and grabbed the rights to University of Chicago halfback Jay Berwanger, who had just won college football's first Heisman Trophy. (The Eagles traded the rights to Berwanger to the Bears, however, and he never played pro football.)

 Touchdown man: In his 11-year career Don Hutson averaged 9 touchdown catches per season. His 99 touchdown receptions was a record for 44 years.

But the immediate future belonged to Halas, who never deviated from his quest for football perfection. The Bears had prevailed in 1932 using a T-formation offense altered by Coach Ralph Jones, who split the ends and halfbacks wider and added a man in motion. When Jones resigned after winning the 1932 title, Halas took over and led the 1933 Bears to a 23-21 victory over the Giants in the NFL's first scheduled championship game.

Halas' Bears would use the innovative offense to procure six Western Division titles and three more NFL championships over the next decade. The centerpiece for his so-called Monsters of the Midway was Nagurski, but a steady stream of talent flowed into Chicago. Elusive Beattie Feathers became the NFL's first 1,000-yard rusher in 1934. Lineman George Musso was fearsome on both sides of the ball. Quarterback Sid Luckman arrived in 1939 to take the ever-evolving "Split-T" to a new level of sophistication.

In 1940, Luckman and the Bears lifted the NFL to new heights of awareness. Avenging an earlier loss to Washington, the Bears posted a stunning 73-0 championship game victory over the Redskins, a still-standing NFL record for domination. It was the first championship game broadcast nationally on radio.

But Halas did not have the corner on talent. Slingin' Sammy Baugh arrived in Washington in 1937 and set the standards by which future passers would be judged. Don Hutson, generally considered one of the greatest pass-catchers of all time, joined the Packers in 1935 to team with passers Arnie Herber and Cecil Isbell and fullback Clarke Hinkle. Byron (Whizzer) White, who would go on to greater fame as a U.S. Supreme

The draft, which would become an NFL institution and force teams to build and expand coaching and scouting staffs, was not the only innovation of the period. The first of 42 College All-Star Games, which pitted a team of collegiate all-stars against the defending NFL champion at Chicago's Soldier Field, was played in 1934. The league adopted a standard 12-game schedule in 1936, and it played its first postseason Pro Bowl game in 1939.

Prosperity was becoming more than a George Halas pipedream. By the end of the decade, every team had its own radio outlet, and television had experimented with its first NFL telecast. More than a million spectators passed

Two-way star: Washington's Sammy Baugh was the NFL's passing leader in 1943, but he also set an NFL record that season, making four interceptions in a game.

through turnstiles in 1939—an NFL first.

The NFL also completed the decade without Carr, who died in 1939. The league launched a search that eventually led to its first commissioner—Elmer Layden of "Four Horsemen" fame.

WAR AND PEACE

Success wouldn't be that easy. The NFL's fast-paced rise to national awareness was halted on December 7, 1941, when Japanese planes launched their surprise attack on Pearl Harbor and thrust the U.S. into World War II. By 1943, professional football had been stripped of its best athletes and those who remained were Sunday performers who spent the rest of the week in war-related activities.

That the NFL was able to continue play was because of President Franklin D. Roosevelt's belief that American sports provided a necessary recreational outlet for a war-weary society. He told baseball and football officials to carry on in whatever manner possible.

The NFL did so—creatively. The Rams suspended operations in 1943, while Pittsburgh and Philadelphia merged into one team called the "Steagles." The Rams returned in 1944, the "Steagles" disbanded and the Boston Yanks joined the NFL. But membership remained at ten, as the Steelers and Cardinals merged into "Card-Pitt."

When the fighting ended in 1945 and athletes returned from Europe and the South Pacific, the NFL found itself embroiled in a different kind of war. Three times in its history the NFL had survived challenges from short-lived rival circuits calling themselves the American Football League. But suddenly there was a new kid on the block—with deep pockets and far-reaching ideas.

Not only was the All-America Football Conference ready and willing to outbid the NFL for new talent, it was willing to take players who wanted to jump from existing rosters. And the AAFC took great pride in the "All-America" portion of its title. Indeed, the eight-team AAFC fielded West Coast franchises in San Francisco (49ers) and Los Angeles (Dons) in 1946, its inaugural season.

The AAFC threat presented serious problems, but its overall impact was positive. When the war ended, former college players, collegians with eligibility remaining and returning veterans formed a talent pool big enough to stock several leagues. And all were eager to play because the AAFC was forcing the NFL to revise its conservative salary structure.

The AAFC also forced the NFL to think bigger. After Dan Reeves watched rookie quarterback Bob Waterfield lead his Cleveland Rams to a 15-14 championship game victory over the Redskins in 1945, he packed up his team and moved to Los Angeles. With air travel and radio advances linking the country from coast to coast, marketing and major population centers suddenly became priority considerations. And the NFL, with Bell now running the show as the commissioner, became aware of image as well as bottom lines.

Ottomatic: Cleveland quarterback Otto Graham's physical and leadership skills carried through his ten seasons in the All-America Football Conference and National Football League.

The AAFC, stocked with quality players, provided entertaining football for four seasons. But it couldn't get past one unfortunate flaw in its game plan—the Cleveland Browns were too good. The star-studded Browns, who outdrew the Rams, compiled a 47-4-3 record and won all four league championships. Their success was a legacy that would not die with the AAFC.

When a peace treaty finally was signed after the 1949 season, the AAFC folded and the NFL absorbed three of its teams: the Browns, 49ers and Baltimore Colts. The bigger and stronger NFL, featuring 13 teams and a myriad of new stars, was ready for a new decade and another period of prosperity.

A MASTER BUILDER

When Paul Brown was asked to build and coach the new AAFC franchise in Cleveland, he was assured there would be plenty of money and no front-office interference. The AAFC, and the rest of the pro football world, was in deep trouble.

Brown, a former Ohio State and Great Lakes Naval Station coach, began building a football machine that would become the toast of the new league and a city that had refused to embrace the NFL's Rams. His greatest gift was talent assessment and he quickly loaded his roster with future Hall of Famers.

Quarterback Otto Graham, whom Brown had watched play at Northwestern, became the heart and soul of a team that included tackle/kicker Lou Groza, fullback Marion Motley, guard Bill Willis, receivers Dante Lavelli, Mac Speedie and Dub Jones and center Frank Gatski. The Browns were solid offensively and defensively, superbly coached by the innovative and detail-minded Brown and confident they could continue their winning ways as members of the NFL.

Few NFL proponents believed they could, including Bell, who scheduled the Browns to play a 1950 season-opening game at Philadelphia. The powerful Eagles were preparing to defend consecutive NFL championships.

It wasn't pretty. The Eagles, playing without injured 1,000-yard rusher Steve Van Buren, were helpless to stop the Browns' sophisticated passing attack and fell meekly, 35-10. The game was viewed by 70,000 stunned fans.

"We really bristled that night," Brown recalled years later. "We had been storing up steam for four years, waiting for a crack at the

The best? Johnny Unitas threw 290 touchdown passes, passed for 40,239 yards, and tossed at least one scoring pass in 47 consecutive games.

National League. When we exploded, there was no stopping us. The Cleveland team that day was the best I ever saw on a given day—anywhere, in any kind of competition."

The AAFC upstarts, competing in the American Conference of the realigned NFL, went on to post a 10-2 record, losing twice to the Giants. But the Browns avenged those losses by defeating the New Yorkers, 8-3, in a conference playoff battle and completed their first-season title run with a 30-28 victory over the Rams. The Browns were undisputed kings of professional football—and they were just getting started.

They captured the next five conference crowns and two more NFL championships. The Browns closed their incredible run (ten consecutive championship game appearances in two leagues) with victories over Detroit and Los Angeles in 1954 and 1955 and then said farewell to Graham, who retired with the greatest success record in pro football history.

As Graham bowed out, a worthy successor to his legacy arrived. Johnny Unitas, who would go on to shatter virtually every NFL passing record over an outstanding 18-year career, joined such talented signal-callers as Bob Waterfield, Norm Van Brocklin, Bobby Layne and Y.A. Tittle.

Unitas wasn't the only arrival of note. The Browns reloaded their backfield with the selection of Syracuse star Jim Brown in the 1957 draft and the second-year star rewarded them a year later by rushing

CROSSING THE COLOR LINE

Jackie Robinson has become an American hero for breaking baseball's color barrier in 1947 with the Brooklyn Dodgers. But lost in Robinson's shadow was the desegregation of professional football, which had quietly begun a year earlier when Cleveland Coach Paul Brown signed fullback Marion Motley and guard Bill Willis to play for his All-America Football Conference team and Rams Owner Dan Reeves signed halfback Kenny Washington and end Woody Strode for his team's first season in Los Angeles.

Reeves' action ended a 12-season period without black players and other teams quickly followed suit. Whereas baseball had not permitted blacks in its game since the 1880s, the NFL had employed a few black performers as late as 1933.

The most celebrated early NFL blacks were halfback Fritz Pollard, who played and coached for a number of teams in the 1920s, and end Paul Robeson, who played three seasons (1920-22) and later pursued a successful acting career. Tackle Duke Slater played for a decade (1922-31) and halfback Joe Lillard was the last black to play (1932-33) before 1946.

for an NFL-record 1,527 yards. The Packers changed their sagging fortunes in the late 1950s when they drafted a quarterback named Bart Starr and hired Vince Lombardi as their coach.

But the defining event of the decade was played out before a national television audience in 1958 when Unitas' Colts met the Giants for the NFL championship at New York's Yankee Stadium. What the game lacked in artistry it made up for with drama and nail-biting emotion—in the media hub of North America.

The game was made to order for publicity-minded NFL officials.

Unitas, who passed for 361 yards and a touchdown, led the Colts on a desperation 73-yard fourth-quarter drive that resulted in Steve Myhra's game-tying 20-yard field goal that forced the first sudden-death overtime in NFL history. The Colts recorded a 23-17 victory when Alan Ameche ran one yard for a touchdown ending "the greatest game of all time" 8:15 into the extra period.

But the NFL's fourth decade would not end on such a positive note. The league, which had survived the challenges of three American Football Leagues and the All-American Football Conference in its first 30 years, was jolted by the 1959 announcement that Dallas businessman Lamar Hunt was forming a new rival circuit that would begin play in 1960. The eight-team league would be called the American Football League.

SURVIVAL OF THE FITTEST

The NFL received another jolt late in the 1959 season when Commissioner Bell died of a heart attack while watching an Eagles-Steelers game. A new, creative mind would be needed to guide professional football through a turbulent and costly era.

It took 23 ballots before Rams General Manager Pete Rozelle was offered the job as a compromise candidate in 1960. Rozelle accepted

the challenge, moved his office to New York and began drawing the blueprint for a prosperous future. But Rozelle's early road to success would be bumpy and difficult.

The AFL, with Hunt as its president and Joe Foss as its first commissioner, quickly made it clear the NFL was facing a long, expensive battle. The new league held its first player draft in November 1959, touching off a bidding war for college talent, and then signed a five-year television contract with ABC. The NFL, in an effort to claim virgin territory, quickly placed new franchises in Dallas and Minneapolis and moved the Cardinals from Chicago to St Louis. The AFL butted heads with the NFL in New York, Los Angeles and Dallas while claiming new markets in Boston, Denver, Houston, Oakland and Buffalo.

But the real war was fought in the trenches after each year's college draft. The AFL made painful inroads and the price of football talent shot up. Its first big prize was former Louisiana State halfback

  Long-time leader: Pete Rozelle was the NFL Commissioner from 1960 to 1989, a period of unprecedented growth in the league.

Above average: Cleveland's Jim Brown was the NFL's rushing leader eight times in nine seasons. His 5.22 yards per carry average is another NFL record.

had produced long-term benefits.

"Looking back, the timing was very right for there to be a second league," Hunt recalled. "The AFL helped popularize the game on a national basis. The game had been centered in the northern and eastern part of the country. We took football to a lot of new areas. The AFL made it a national game and nurtured the rivalry that ultimately created the Super Bowl."

It also more than doubled the NFL's size, produced innovative changes that helped attract fans, improved player salaries and benefits, brought about a whopping increase in television revenue and turned the sport into a big, profitable business.

While the young AFL was attracting fans with its pass-first, no-defense philosophy, the NFL was trying to cope with another kind of monster. After losing to the Eagles, 17-13, in the 1960 championship game, Vince Lombardi's Packers defeated the Giants in 1961 and 1962, the Browns in 1965 and the Cowboys in 1966 and 1967. It was the most dominating run in NFL history.

But of more importance, the Starr-led Packers upheld the NFL's honor in the first two AFL-NFL championship games, battles that later would be called Super Bowls. The Packers overpowered the AFC-champion Kansas City Chiefs in Super Bowl I, 35-10, and blew away the Raiders in Super Bowl II, 33-14.

Smug NFL patrons smiled broadly in anticipation of what the powerful Colts, 34-0 NFL Championship Game winners over the Browns in 1968, would do to the upstart Jets in Super Bowl III. And they laughed out loud when the brash Namath announced, "The Jets will win on Sunday, I guarantee it." But AFL fans were the ones laughing when Namath and the Jets delivered a stunning 16-7 victory, earning the league some much needed respect. When the AFL Chiefs followed with a 23-7 victory over the NFL Vikings in Super Bowl IV, the AFL began the merger with heads held high.

By the end of the 1960s, the NFL's tentacles had expanded into the Deep South (Atlanta, New Orleans and Miami) and the Super Bowl was being hailed as the greatest show on Earth. The new decade would begin with the 26-team NFL locked into a four-year, $150-million television contract that included $8 million from ABC for a 13-game Monday Night Football package. The NFL was on a roll.

ONWARD AND UPWARD

The NFL, buoyed by record-setting attendance in 1969, prepared for its first 26-team season with a sense of relief and optimism. The new-look league would begin in 1970 with two 13-team conferences: The AFL newcomers would join the Browns, Colts and Steelers in the American Football Conference; the other NFL holdovers would compete in the National Football Conference.

But before the first pass could be thrown, a new problem surfaced. NFL players, aware of the big money suddenly flowing into coffers around the league, threatened to sit out the season unless management allocated money for their pension fund and other benefits. The surprisingly strong union maneuver resulted in a major boost to the pension fund and a contract agreement that would insure peace until at least 1974. But the player-management bickering was a portent of things to come.

That became obvious when renegotiations started in 1974 amid renewed strike threats and legal hassles. At issue was the so-called "Rozelle Rule," which gave the commissioner the right to decide compensation for free agents and thus discouraged teams from pursuing opposing players. When a federal court struck down the "Rozelle Rule" as illegal, the owners and players finally reached a contract agreement in 1977, creating a new free-agent system that proved equally as restrictive. The players were locked in for another five years.

Despite the labor unrest, the game prospered on the field and in the eyes of a growing fan base. The early part of the decade belonged to

and Heisman Trophy winner Billy Cannon. And a Who's Who list of big-name stars followed: safety Johnny Robinson, tackle Ron Mix, center Jim Otto, wide receiver Lance Alworth, defensive tackle Buck Buchanan, running back Mike Garrett, linebacker Bobby Bell, wide receiver Fred Biletnikoff and many more.

But the AFL's biggest coup occurred in 1965 when New York Jets Owner Sonny Werblin, badly in need of a star attraction to steady his wobbling franchise, landed quarterback Joe Namath. Broadway Joe, charismatic and unpredictable, was enthusiastically embraced by the New York City media and fans.

The war raged for seven years before a truce was called in 1966. On June 8, Rozelle announced a merger agreement that called for a championship game between the rival leagues after the 1966 season, a combined draft and interleague preseason play in 1967, and a common schedule beginning in 1970. All existing franchises would be retained.

As with the AAFC merger 17 years earlier, the bitterly fought war

The 2,003-YARD MAN

As the 1973 season progressed, the football world watched intently to see if Buffalo's OJ Simpson could top the greatest one-season rushing performance in NFL history—Jim Brown's 1963 mark of 1,863 yards.

And with two games remaining, it appeared Simpson had a pretty fair shot at history. He needed to total 280 yards against the New England Patriots and New York Jets to pass Brown and he had rushed for 250 against the Patriots in the Bills' season opener.

But Simpson took his challenge a step further. He exploded for 219 yards against New England on December 9 and closed with a 200-yard outburst against the Jets. Not only had he topped Brown, he had crossed the previously unthinkable barrier of 2,000 yards. Here are Simpson's game-by-game totals:

	ATT.	YARDS
NEW ENGLAND	29	250
SAN DIEGO	22	103
NY JETS	24	123
PHILADELPHIA	27	171
BALTIMORE	22	166
MIAMI	14	55
KANSAS CITY	39	157
NEW ORLEANS	20	79
CINCINNATI	20	99
MIAMI	20	120
BALTIMORE	15	124
ATLANTA	24	137
NEW ENGLAND	22	219
NEW YORK JETS	34	200
TOTAL	332	2,003

Perfect season: Miami Dolphins (left to right) Larry Csonka, Jim Kiick and Coach Don Shula look on as the defense keeps the perfect season intact.

Coach Don Shula and his Miami Dolphins; the later years to Coach Chuck Noll's Pittsburgh Steelers.

The Dolphins, featuring the power running of Larry Csonka, Jim Kiick and Mercury Morris, the crafty quarterbacking of Bob Griese and a "No-Name Defense" that swarmed and stuffed opposing offenses, reached national prominence in 1971 when they captured their first AFC crown before losing to Dallas in the Super Bowl. But the 1972 Dolphins would not be denied—by anybody.

They crafted a 14-0 regular season, beat Cleveland and Pittsburgh in the playoffs and completed the NFL's first perfect season (17-0) with a 14-7 victory over Washington in Super Bowl VII. The Dolphins were not perfect in 1973, but they were good enough to defeat Minnesota, 24-7, in Super Bowl VIII. The closest thing to 1973 perfection was the performance of Buffalo running back O J Simpson, who became the NFL's first 2,000-yard rusher.

The Dolphins' grip was released the next season when a "Steel Curtain" dropped manacingly over the NFL. The Steelers, a long-dormant franchise, rode the strong arm of Terry Bradshaw, the running of Franco Harris and a stifling defense featuring tackle Mean Joe Greene and linebackers Jack Ham and Jack Lambert to four Super Bowl titles in the next six years.

The Miami and Pittsburgh influences plus the threat of another rival league in 1974 resulted in changes that would make the game more entertaining and exciting. By mid-decade, the high-scoring, pass-happy days of the 1960s were but a distant memory as coaches gravitated toward power offenses and a safer, more-conservative defensive philosophy. When the World Football League formed, however the NFL adopted rule changes that would force excitement back into its stodgy product.

The most far-reaching rule was sudden-death overtime to eliminate ties. But the NFL also moved the goal posts back ten yards to the end lines to cut back on field goals, limited defensive backs to

one bump of eligible pass receivers and reduced the penalty for offensive holding.

The WFL threat was short and expensive. The new league did lure a number of stars with big-money inducements, but midway through its second season, facing huge debts and no promise of future success, the WFL folded.

AN INTERNATIONAL LOOK

From 1986, when the NFL launched its American Bowl series with a game between Dallas and Chicago at London's Wembley Stadium, to 1995, when the NFL and FOX Broadcasting resumed the World League featuring an all-European lineup of teams, professional football literally has come a long way.

That first American Bowl drew more than 82,000 fans and became so popular that the series was expanded to include games in Tokyo, Berlin, Barcelona and Mexico City. The London response was so strong that NFL Properties opened an office there in 1989 and launched a program of international sales and licensing that now tops $375 million. NFL interest is so high throughout the world that weekly telecasts now reach more than 150 countries and recent Super Bowls have been watched by an overseas audience estimated at 750 million.

The success of the American Bowl also led to formation of the World League, which in 1991 became the first league to operate on two continents. The league suspended play after the 1992 season, but reappeared as a six-team circuit with a 10-week schedule in April 1995. The new World League, which opened with franchises in Amsterdam, Dusseldorf, Edinburgh, Barcelona, Frankfurt and London, requires each team to have at least seven European players and one European assistant coach.

FORWARD VISION

The NFL, bolstered by expansion to Tampa and Seattle in 1976 and an increase to a 16-game regular-season format in 1978, played to rave reviews as the 1980s dawned. Record attendance figures were posted and the old guard was passing its mantle to a new wave of rising stars. Such former crowd-pleasers as Namath, Simpson, Harris and Roger Staubach were either gone or fading fast. Players like running backs Walter Payton, Tony Dorsett and Marcus Allen, tight end Kellen Winslow, wide receiver Jerry Rice and quarterbacks Joe Montana, John Elway and Dan Marino were rising to prominence.

But the game was not without problems. First the issue of franchise stability crept into the spotlight, frustrating and bewildering the fans. Then labor scuffling turned into a war that tested the fabric of the game.

Little did Raiders Owner Al Davis realize the can of worms he was opening when, upset because the league turned down his bid to move from Oakland to Los Angeles, he took his case to court in 1980 and two years later won a long, bitter battle that weakened the NFL's power over its franchises. Davis' victory had a trickling effect. In 1984, the Colts moved from Baltimore to Indianapolis and four years later the Cardinals left St. Louis for Phoenix. The dam broke in 1995 and 1996 when the Los Angeles Rams relocated to St. Louis, the Raiders returned to Oakland, the Cleveland Browns made a gut-wrenching shift to Baltimore (where they became the Ravens) and the Oilers were making final plans for a move to Nashville in 1995. The promise of new stadiums and increased income was too good to ignore and owners could not resist overtures from football-hungry cities.

Labor took center stage in 1982 when negotiations for a new basic agreement broke down and the players staged a 57-day in-season strike. But owners were prepared in 1987 when the players walked out again after Week 2 of the season. They continued their schedule using replacement players and the union, stung by players crossing the picket line, gave in after 24 days.

The labor friction finally eased in 1993 when owners and players agreed to a far-reaching contract that would keep the game on the field until at least 1999. The owners got a salary cap and the players got unrestricted free agency after four years and the promise of higher salaries. Everybody reveled in a 1993 TV contract for $4.35 billion.

Despite a steady flow of off-field distractions, the game flourished. The San Francisco 49ers, with Coach Bill Walsh and quarterback Montana directing a controlled-passing attack—the West Coast offense—won their first Super Bowl after the 1981 season and began a record-setting journey that would culminate with a fifth Super Bowl victory after the 1994 season under the direction of Coach George Seifert and quarterback Steve Young. But the 49ers were merely the kings of an NFC that dominated its AFC brethren from 1981-95. The Redskins and Cowboys won three Super Bowls apiece, the Giants won two and the Bears one. The Cowboys earned their three titles in a four-year span from 1992-95.

By the mid-1990s, the NFL was displaying resiliency amid prosperity and confusion. It had survived yet another rival league (the three-season United States Football League) and expanded to 30 teams with new franchises in Charlotte, NC, and Jacksonville, Fla. Rozelle, the commissioner who led the league to great prosperity, retired and was replaced by Paul Tagliabue, who turned his sights to foreign markets. But as Tagliabue established international credibility with the proliferation of the American Bowl and the creation of the World League, he was concerned about the number of franchise moves.

It was amid such activity that football fans bid farewell to one of the game's great legends. Dolphins Coach Don Shula, who had posted an all-time record of 347 victories over seven seasons with the Baltimore Colts and 26 with Miami, retired. He was replaced after the 1995 season by Jimmy Johnson, the man who had led the Cowboys to their 1992 and 1993 Super Bowl victories.

Everybody Wants to Play

In the long history of the National Football League, not one individual has ever won an NFL championship or a Super Bowl. Teams win championships; individuals win accolades and honors. Scoring and passing titles are showy and nice, but they don't fit the ego quite like a Super Bowl ring.

Just ask Detroit's Barry Sanders if he would trade his 1994 rushing title for a championship. San Francisco quarterback Steve Young shrugs when asked about his four straight passing titles, but his eyes light up when he recalls his team's victory in Super Bowl XXIX.

Team success is the backbone of all sports competition, but it's also the most difficult level to attain. Finding talented players to fill roster spots is one thing; blending them into cohesive, working units is another. Once an organization does taste success, sustaining it over an extended period is the ultimate test of its leadership and coaching.

That's an especially difficult task in professional football, where a "team" consists of 45 players divided into three distinct units—offense, defense and special teams. Basketball coaches have to coordinate the efforts of 12 players, all of whom play both offense and defense; baseball managers have 25. The sheer numbers, combined with the physical toll football takes on its players, explains why the 1960s-era Green Bay Packers, perhaps the NFL's greatest dynasty, lasted only seven years.

Vince Lombardi was the architect of that glorious run and he did it with old-fashioned principles—discipline, commitment to winning and a demanding work schedule. He sought out players who would embrace his philosophy, molded his offense and defense into smooth-running machines that valued efficiency over individual glory and instilled his hatred for losing. Lombardi, a demanding, forceful and sometimes-abrasive personality, translated his intensity into five NFL championships in seven seasons.

Lombardi's methods were not all that much different from those used by George Halas, Chicago's Papa Bear, who built the "Monsters of the Midway" powerhouse that won five NFL titles and appeared in three more championship games from 1932-43. But they were light years removed from the coaching innovations of Paul Brown, who directed the Cleveland Browns to four consecutive All-America Football Conference championships and three titles in the team's first six NFL seasons.

Brown, considered one of the great talent judges in football history, was analytical, precise and innovative. He was a teacher as much as a coach. And he was always the gentleman, although his calm, stately exterior was only a cover for the competitive fire that burned inside. His methods might have been different from Lombardi's, but his philosophies were strikingly similar.

All coaches must be astute judges of talent, but successful coaches take their assessment abilities beyond the field. Like Halas, Lombardi and Brown, they must be able to spot character players and overachievers who often bring more to the team concept than their more athletically gifted competitors. Coaches like Don Shula, Chuck Noll, Bill Walsh and Jimmy Johnson have parlayed their special abilities into more recent successful runs that are especially impressive in the context of rising player salaries.

Shula led the Miami Dolphins to three consecutive Super Bowl appearances from 1971-73 and back-to-back championships (1972-73). Noll's Pittsburgh Steelers came close to matching the Packers with four Super Bowl championships in six years from 1974-79. Walsh was the architect of the San Francisco 49ers express that rolled to four Super Bowl titles in the 1980s (three under his coaching), and Johnson brought the Dallas Cowboys back from the dead to win consecutive Super Bowls after the 1992 and 1993 seasons. Super-

fur a Winner

Division rivals: Minnesota's rivalry with Green Bay is one of the most intense in the NFL. Here Cris Carter is tackled by a Packer defender.

Bowl winning coaches like Joe Gibbs and Bill Parcells also have brought winning attitudes to organizations that previously lacked direction.

Several common threads run through the fabric of football's greatest teams. Foremost is the presence of a quarterback more gifted as a leader than athletically. Chicago's Sid Luckman, Cleveland's Otto Graham and Green Bay's Bart Starr were not the most talented passers or runners—but they knew how to win. So did Miami's Bob Griese, Pittsburgh's Terry Bradshaw, San Francisco's Joe Montana

and Dallas' Troy Aikman. Montana was a third-round draft pick; Starr came in the 17th round. Griese's statistics have been dwarfed by current Dolphins quarterback Dan Marino, but Marino has never won a championship.

The great teams also have big-play running backs and, of course, defenses that operate with machine-like efficiency—a characteristic common to every winning team in every sport.

In football, like in basketball, baseball and hockey, such efficiency is called teamwork. It produces championships, not just gaudy statistics.

Baltimore Ravens

A BROWNOUT IN CLEVELAND

It became official in February 1996. Art Modell was granted league approval to move his Cleveland Browns, one of the most storied franchises in football history, to Baltimore. Modell's decision was a lesson in economic realities.

But it also was a costly and painful sacrifice. The two things he was forced to leave behind cannot be measured in monetary value: the venerable Browns nickname and a rich history that was built around one of football's greatest dynasties.

That dynasty was the 1946 creation of master football architect Paul Brown, who put together a star-studded post-World War II team that dominated the All-America Football Conference for four seasons (47-4-3 record) and reached the championship game in each of its first six NFL seasons, winning three titles.

The Browns were quarterbacked by Otto Graham, who guided them to 10 consecutive title games, and Graham's supporting cast included such stars as fullback Marion Motley, guard Bill Willis, receivers Dante Lavelli and Mac Speedie, halfback Dub Jones, center Frank Gatski, and tackle/kicker Lou Groza.

That talent and success level would never be matched, but the future Browns did have their moments—and stars. The 1964 team gave Cleveland its fourth NFL championship and the Graham-Motley traditions have wound like a thread through franchise history.

Motley passed the baton to such running machines as Jim Brown, Leroy Kelly, Greg Pruitt and Mike Pruitt, who combined for 17 1,000-yard seasons. Graham was followed by a talented line of passing quarterbacks—Milt Plum, Frank Ryan, Brian Sipe and Bernie Kosar.

Even in the 31 years after their last title, the Browns continued to win. They finished .500 or better 20 times, lost three NFL title games and dropped three heart-breaking AFC Championship Games to Denver. The 1986 and 1987 disappointments came under the direction of Coach Marty Schottenheimer; Bud Carson was at the controls in 1989.

Bill Belichick's 1994 Browns, featuring Vinny Testaverde at quarterback and such big-play defenders as cornerback Antonio Langham, safety Eric Turner and end Rob Burnett, posted an 11-5 record before losing to Pittsburgh in a divisional playoff game.

But the 1995 Browns tumbled to 5-11 as they battled the distractions of the impending move. Now the players face the challenge of establishing a new history in Baltimore under new coach Ted Marchibroda

Meanwhile, the Browns will be reactivated in Cleveland in 1997 with that team assuming the club's rich history.

FACTS AND FIGURES

CONFERENCE/DIVISION	AFC Central
FIRST YEAR IN NFL	1966
STADIUM/CAPACITY/SURFACE	Memorial Stadium (60,000) /Grass
FORMER CITIES/NICKNAMES	None
NFL CHAMPIONSHIPS	None
SUPER BOWL CHAMPIONSHIPS	None

PLAYING RECORD	W	L	T	PCT
Regular Season	374	266	10	.583
Playoffs (23 Appearances)	11	19	0	.367

Cover up: Cornerback Antonio Langham is young, fast and rates among the league's best defensive backs in one-on-one coverage.

Buffalo Bills

FOUR'S NOT A CHARM

You can't really blame Buffalo players and fans for feeling a little testy. In a world where success is measured by recent impressions, the Bills are fighting a losing battle. They have won more games in the 1990s than every team except San Francisco and Dallas. From 1990 through 1993, they compiled a 49-15 regular-season record, won three AFC East Division titles and captured four AFC championships. They became the first team to play in four consecutive Super Bowls-and that's the catch. They lost all four.

So instead of being hailed as one of the dominant teams of football history, the Bills' accomplishments have been lost in the massive shadow of their frustration. That frustration had been building for more than 20 years.

The Bills, an original member of the American Football League, have been looking for an NFL championship since becoming a league member in 1970. Buffalo had captured consecutive AFL titles in 1964 and 1965 under the leadership of Coach Lou Saban and quarterback Jack Kemp, but success would be more difficult in the expanded NFL. From 1970-1987, the Bills qualified for the playoffs only three times and each of those postseason appearances was brief.

The 1970s were memorable primarily because of the rushing feats of OJ Simpson, who ran for an incredible 2,003 yards in 1973. But he led the Bills to only three winning seasons and one playoff appearance. The 1980s were spent rebuilding a franchise that was drifting without an apparent game plan.

It wasn't until Coach Marv Levy arrived in 1986 that the momentum shifted. Levy began molding his explosive no-huddle offense around quarterback Jim Kelly, a 1986 signee from the United States Football League, and several key draft picks—running back Thurman Thomas, wide receiver Andre Reed, and tackle Howard Ballard. Defensively, the Bills were anchored by end Bruce Smith and linebackers Cornelius Bennett and Darryl Talley.

That talent core was good enough to get the Bills to the "Show," but getting there was only half the battle. Their failure to win (they were outscored 139-73 in their four Super Bowls) was anguishing for players and fans alike.

The Bills stumbled to a 7-9 record in 1994 and failed to qualify for the playoffs for the first time since 1987. But with critics sniping and fans reading last rites, the 1995 Bills bounced back to post a 10-6 record, claim another division title and win a first-round playoff game. Whether Kelly, Thomas, Smith and company can duplicate such heroics while young talent is fed into the mix will determine the franchise's future course.

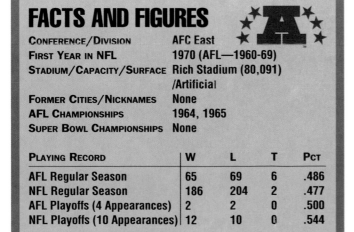

FACTS AND FIGURES

CONFERENCE/DIVISION	AFC East
FIRST YEAR IN NFL	1970 (AFL—1960-69)
STADIUM/CAPACITY/SURFACE	Rich Stadium (80,091) /Artificial
FORMER CITIES/NICKNAMES	None
AFL CHAMPIONSHIPS	1964, 1965
SUPER BOWL CHAMPIONSHIPS	None

PLAYING RECORD	W	L	T	PCT
AFL Regular Season	65	69	6	.486
NFL Regular Season	186	204	2	.477
AFL Playoffs (4 Appearances)	2	2	0	.500
NFL Playoffs (10 Appearances)	12	10	0	.544

 Hands on: Quarterback Jim Kelly and the no-huddle offense have taken the Bills to the brink of four championships.

Cincinnati Bengals

BACK TO THE FUTURE

They were fast out of the box. They were consistent. And they were resilient. The pre-1990s Bengals were all of the above-and they tantalized their fans with two Super Bowl near-misses. But aside from a 9-7 record in 1990 and a hope-producing 7-9 comeback in 1995, the current decade has been a lost cause. Those two seasons sandwiched 3-13, 5-11, 3-13 and 3-13 campaigns that frustrated long-faithful fans who remember Paul Brown's expansion masterpiece.

Brown, a master football architect, created the Bengals as an American Football League entry in 1968. His newborn team flourished quickly, winning its first AFC Central Division championship in its third season-its first under the AFL-NFL merger agreement. After a 4-10 dip in 1971, Brown had enough talent in place to assure success for the immediate future.

With 1971 draftee Ken Anderson at quarterback, Boobie Clark and Essex Johnson in the backfield, Isaac Curtis at wide receiver and linebacker Jim LeClair anchoring the defense, the Bengals posted winning records in three of the next four seasons, including another AFC Central title.

Bill Johnson took over for Brown in 1976 and posted winning records in his first two seasons. But back-to-back four-12 marks prompted the Bengals to turn matters over to Forrest Gregg. In 1981, the Bengals, playing in their new tiger-striped uniforms, soared to a 12-4 record, defeated San Diego in the AFC Championship Game and extended San Francisco in Super Bowl XVI before dropping a 26-21 decision.

But with Anderson, Curtis, LeClair, Pete Johnson, and many others nearing the end of their careers, the Bengals were forced to reload. Boomer Esiason replaced Anderson, Eddie Brown replaced Curtis, holdovers Anthony Muñoz and Max Montoya led a dominating offensive line, and Ickey Woods and James Brooks provided a double-threat running tandem. Nose tackle Tim Krumrie, linebacker Reggie Williams and safety David Fulcher became the heart of a stingy defense.

Sam Wyche replaced Gregg in 1984, and by 1988 the Bengals rose up to claim another AFC championship and a second Super Bowl berth. They lost a 20-16 heart-breaker when the 49ers scored a touchdown with 34 seconds remaining.

Wyche posted 8-8 and 9-7 records before sagging to 3-13 and losing his job to Dave Shula, the son of former Miami Coach Don Shula. Dave Shula, like his team, is young (37) and learning.

Quarterback Jeff Blake, wideout Carl Pickens and defensive tackle Dan Wilkinson were quick studies in 1995 and Shula is hoping running back Ki-Jana Carter, the first overall pick of the 1995 draft, can rebound from a serious knee injury. If so, the decade might have a happy ending.

 Hard charging: Dan Wilkinson is the massive anchor on the Bengal's young defensive line.

FACTS AND FIGURES

CONFERENCE/DIVISION	AFC Central
FIRST YEAR IN NFL	1970 (AFL 1968-69)
STADIUM/CAPACITY/SURFACE	Riverfront Stadium (60,389) /Artificial
FORMER CITIES/NICKNAMES	None
AFL CHAMPIONSHIPS	None
SUPER BOWL CHAMPIONSHIPS	None

PLAYING RECORD	W	L	T	PCT
AFL Regular Season	7	20	1	.268
NFL Regular Season	185	207	0	.472
AFL Playoffs	0	0	0	.000
NFL Playoffs (7 Appearances)	5	7	0	.417

Denver Broncos

A ROCKY MOUNTAIN HIGH

Denver fans with short memories might have trouble recalling professional football without John Elway. Those with long memories might not want to. Elway, the strong-armed former Stanford quarterback, has completed 13 impressive seasons with the Broncos—exactly half of their NFL existence. He has led the team to seven playoff berths and three Super Bowls while garnering adulation as one of the great late-game quarterbacks of all time.

Those who do remember life without Elway need go back no further than 1977, when Red Miller's "Orange Crush" Broncos captured the franchise's first AFC Western Division championship, earned its first AFC title and lost its first Super Bowl—a 27-10 cakewalk for the Dallas Cowboys. That feverish season, the first playoff appearance for a franchise that dated back to 1960 as a charter member of the American Football League, was orchestrated by overachieving quarterback Craig Morton and a "crushing" defense featuring end Lyle Alzado, linebackers Randy Gradishar and Tom Jackson and nose tackle Rubin Carter.

How bad were the pre-1977 Broncos? In 17 seasons, the franchise had posted only three winning records. But when Elway arrived in 1983, a lust for winning quickly gave way to loftier concerns.

Blessed with a shotgun arm, uncanny scrambling ability and a knack for late-game heroics, Elway led the Dan Reeves-coached Broncos on a playoff run that proved to be both exciting and frustrating. They reached the Super Bowl after the 1986, 1987 and 1989 seasons, but dropped 39-20, 42-10 and 55-10 decisions to the Giants, Redskins and 49ers. The Broncos joined Minnesota as the only four-time Super Bowl losers—a club that later would include Buffalo.

With the aging and retirement of such supporting players as running back Sammy Winder, wide receivers Steve Watson, Mark Jackson and Ricky Nattiel and defensive players Karl Mecklenburg and Dennis Smith, the Broncos have struggled. Reeves led Denver to another AFC Championship Game in 1991 before being replaced by Wade Phillips, who lost his job to Mike Shanahan after a 7-9 record in 1994.

Shanahan, a former offensive mastermind for the 49ers, has hit the free-agent market in his effort to revive the magic. His defense still needs a lot of work, but Shanahan has 1,000-yard running back Terrell Davis, receivers Anthony Miller and Shannon Sharpe and, of course, a quarterback named Elway.

 On guard: Steve Atwater (27) preaches safety for a Broncos defense that is under reconstruction.

FACTS AND FIGURES

CONFERENCE/DIVISION	AFC West
FIRST YEAR IN NFL	1970 (AFL 1960-69)
STADIUM/CAPACITY/SURFACE	Mile High Stadium (76,273) /Grass
FORMER CITIES/NICKNAMES	None
AFL CHAMPIONSHIPS	None
SUPER BOWL CHAMPIONSHIPS	None

PLAYING RECORD	W	L	T	PCT
AFL Regular Season	39	97	4	.293
NFL Regular Season	217	169	6	.561
AFL Playoffs	0	0	0	.000
NFL Playoffs (10 Appearances)	9	10	0	.474

Houston Oilers

BETTER LUCK NEXT TIME

As enthusiastic young Coach Jeff Fisher tries to rebuild the Huston Oilers, it brings to mind the three successful eras of an inconsistent past. From 1960-62, their first three seasons in the American Football League, the Oilers won consecutive championships and barely missed a third when they lost to the Dallas Texans in the 1962 title game. Those teams featured the passing of George Blanda and the running of 1960 Heisman Trophy winner Billy Cannon.

FACTS AND FIGURES

CONFERENCE/DIVISION	AFC Central
FIRST YEAR IN NFL	1970 (AFL 1960-69)
STADIUM/CAPACITY/SURFACE	Astrodome (59,905)/Artificial
FORMER CITIES/NICKNAMES	None
AFL CHAMPIONSHIPS	1960, 1961
SUPER BOWL CHAMPIONSHIPS	None

PLAYING RECORD	W	L	T	PCT
AFL Regular Season	70	66	4	.514
NFL Regular Season	173	217	2	.444
AFL Playoffs (5 Appearances)	2	3	0	.400
NFL Playoffs (10 Appearances)	7	10	0	.412

From 1978-80, the Bum Phillips-coached Oilers lost to Central Division-rival Pittsburgh in consecutive AFC Championship Games and dropped a first-round playoff contest to Oakland-all teams that went on to win Super Bowls. These Oilers featured quarterback Dan Pastorini and bulldozing running back Earl Campbell, a five-time 1,000-yard rusher.

From 1987-93, the Jerry Glanville and Jack Pardee-coached Oilers won two AFC Central titles and earned seven consecutive playoff appearances. Those teams featured strong-armed Warren Moon throwing to a speedy group of receivers-Webster Slaughter, Ernest Givins, Haywood Jeffires and Drew Hill.

From Blanda to Pastorini to Moon, the Oilers' success has come in different measures. Blanda was a big-play quarterback. Phillips' Oilers were powered by the strong legs of Campbell. The recent Oilers were a high-powered passing offense, operating from 1990-93 in Pardee's Run-and-Shoot offense.

Moon was masterful in the Run-and-Shoot, but the offense was susceptible to occasional shutdowns. The Oilers' defense was big and bruising, but sometimes vulnerable to the big play. Houston fans still shudder at the thought of a 1992 playoff loss to Buffalo in which the Oilers blew a 32-point second-half lead.

The playoff streak unraveled after the 1993 season when Moon was traded to Minnesota and several key players left as free agents. Pardee was fired midway through a 2-14 1994 disaster and Fisher guided the team to a 7-9 revival in 1995—a campaign that ended with rookie quarterback Steve McNair leading the team to victories in the last two games.

Fisher, who discarded the Run-and-Shoot, will have either McNair or veteran Chris Chandler throwing to Willie Davies, Chris Sanders, and running back Todd McNair, and handing off to running back Rodney Thomas. The defense is young and improving. With the team planning to move to Nashville Tennessee, in 1998 the Oilers' fourth winning era could take place in two different states.

The Rifleman: Strong-armed quarterback Steve McNair should become a major factor in every Oilers' game plan.

Indianapolis Colts

THE END OF AN ENIGMA

★ ★ ★ ★ ★ ★ ★ ★ ★ ★ ★ ★ ★ ★

Hope springs eternal for Indianapolis football fans, who for more than a decade paid for their blind faith with frustration and disappointment. But good things come to those who wait and the 1995 Colts erased a lot of bad feelings. After 11 Indianapolis seasons had produced three winning records, 67 victories and one playoff berth, Ted Marchibroda's 1995 team reached the playoffs with a 9-7 record, pulled two upsets and battled Pittsburgh into the final seconds of a heart-breaking AFC Championship Game loss. The resurgence was orchestrated by veteran quarterback Jim Harbaugh, two-time 1,000-yard rusher Marshall Faulk and a young, improving defense.

Success was perfect medicine. Hard times may have followed owner Robert Irsay's move from Baltimore Indianapolis, but lack of success shouldn't suggest lack of effort.

The Colts have used head coaches during their midwest tenure seven times, including new coach Lindy Infante. They traded away a big chunk of their future to get Rams running back Eric Dickerson in 1987. They drafted franchise quarterback Jeff George with the first overall pick in 1990. They drafted defensive lineman Steve Emtman and linebacker Quentin Coryatt with the first and second overall picks of 1992. They grabbed Faulk with the second overall pick of 1994.

Dickerson continued his 1,000-yard ways for three of his Indianapolis seasons, but the Colts could do no better than 9-6. George never could get untracked with the Colts and was traded to Atlanta after the 1993 season. Emtman blew out his knee and Coryatt went down with a wrist injury in their rookie seasons.

Faulk rushed for 1,282 rookie yards and 1,078 in 1995. He remains the centerpiece for new Coach Lindy Infante's ball-control attack and the Colts' closest link to a fabled past in a distant city.

The Baltimore Colts rekindle memories of Johnny Unitas, Lenny Moore, Raymond Berry, Gino Marchetti, Alan Ameche, John Mackey, Tom Matte, Bubba Smith and many other football greats; of 1958 and 1959 NFL championships; of a shocking Super Bowl III loss to Joe Namath and the New York Jets and a vindicating Super Bowl V victory over Dallas; of three consecutive AFC Eastern Division championships in the mid-1970s; of stability and greatness.

Many of today's young Colts probably don't even know about the team's glorious past, but they do understand the need to create special memories for the fans of Indianapolis. Maybe 1995 was the beginning.

Speedy Colt: Marshall Faulk was slowed by injuries in 1995, but he still recorded his second 1,000-yard season.

FACTS AND FIGURES

CONFERENCE/DIVISION	AFC East
FIRST YEAR IN NFL	1953
STADIUM/CAPACITY/SURFACE	RCA Dome (60,127) /Artificial
FORMER CITIES/NICKNAMES	Baltimore Colts (1953-83)
NFL CHAMPIONSHIPS	1958, 1959, 1968, 1970 (Super Bowl)

PLAYING RECORD	W	L	T	Pct
Regular Season	298	309	7	.491
Playoffs (11 Appearances)	10	9	0	.526

Jacksonville Jaguars

FIRST IMPRESSIONS ★★★★★★★★★★★★★★★★★

By NFL expansion standards, the 1995 Jaguars were a veritable powerhouse. Not only did they win four games, more than any previous expansion team, they posted an unprecedented .500 AFC Central Division record, swept division-rival Cleveland and averaged a respectable 17.2 points per game.

But nobody seemed to notice. While Jacksonville was challenging the expansion laws of gravity, the Carolina Panthers were defying them with a first-year 7-9 record and a playoff challenge that came up short on the season's final day.

If Tom Coughlin's Jaguars developed a bit of an inferiority complex, they never showed it on the field. One of their victories was over Super Bowl-bound Pittsburgh and eight of their losses were by 10 or fewer points. They were young, inexperienced and often outmanned, but they never gave an inch.

To put Jacksonville's one-season past and many-season future into perspective consider:

Coughlin used 16 different starting combinations on offense, 12 on defense. His search for the perfect talent blend never ceased. Four 1995 draft picks, offensive tackles Tony Boselli and Brian DeMarco, running back James Stewart and linebacker Bryan Schwartz, started most of Jacksonville's games. When the season ended, the Jaguars had nine former first-round draft picks and 13 rookies on their active roster. The team's average age was 25.5 years.

The first-year team ranked 21st overall in defense and 28th in offense. While the Jaguars aren't on anybody's list of Super Bowl contenders, those numbers and the first-year performances of several key players suggest a bright future.

Coughlin got surprising results from quarterback Mark Brunell, who beat out Steve Beuerlein and passed for 2,168 yards and 15 touchdowns. Brunell, who threw only seven interceptions, also rushed for 480 yards, while averaging 7.2-yard per carry. Other fine performances were turned in by Stewart (525 rushing yards), tight end Pete Mitchell (41 receptions), tackle Boselli and the rest of an offensive line that averaged 6-foot-6, 308 pounds.

Having set the tone with an exciting first-year team, Coughlin is faced now with a difficult question: What can the Jaguars do for an encore? After an aggressive offseason in which the team signed several top free agents, including Steelers Jackie Leon Searce and Oilers linebacker Eddie Robinson, and claimed Chargers running back Natrone Means on waivers, the answer could be plenty.

★★★★★★★★★★★★★

Tony award: Young tackle Tony Roselli, a 1995 No. 2 overall draft pick, was downright offensive for the expansion Jaguars.

FACTS AND FIGURES

CONFERENCE/DIVISION	AFC Central
FIRST YEAR IN NFL	1995
STADIUM/CAPACITY/SURFACE	Jacksonville Municipal Stadium (73,000)/Grass
PLAYING RECORD	4-12, First NFL season

Kansas City Chiefs

RECLAIMING PAST GLORY

This is a tale of two eras. The 1960s Chiefs were an American Football League power, directed by Coach Hank Stram and driven by such performers as quarterback Len Dawson, running back Mike Garrett, wide receiver Otis Taylor, defensive tackle Buck Buchanan, linebackers Willie Lanier and Bobby Bell and defensive back Johnny Robinson. Stram's Team's captured three AFL championships and appeared in two Super Bowls, losing to Green Bay in the inaugural classic and beating Minnesota in the fourth title game.

The Chiefs of the late 1980s and 1990s have been an AFC power, choreographed by Coach Marty Schottenheimer and driven by such performers as quarterbacks Joe Montana and Steve Bono, running backs Christian Okoye and Marcus Allen, wide receiver Lake Dawson, defensive end Neil Smith, linebacker Derrick Thomas, and cornerback Dale Carter. Schottenheimer's Chiefs have reached the playoffs six consecutive seasons and the AFC Championship Game once, but they have not been able to take the final step.

Everything between Stram and Schottenheimer was a blur for loyal Kansas City fans, who suffered through 21 consecutive seasons without a playoff victory and a 12-season stretch with one winning record. The 1970s and early 1980s were as forgettable as the other years are memorable. The Chiefs, started by AFL founder Lamar

FACTS AND FIGURES

CONFERENCE/DIVISION	AFC West
FIRST YEAR IN NFL	1970 (AFL 1960-69)
STADIUM/CAPACITY/SURFACE	Arrowhead Stadium (77,872) /Grass
FORMER CITIES/NICKNAMES	Dallas Texans (1960-62)
AFL CHAMPIONSHIPS	1962, 1966, 1969
SUPER BOWL CHAMPIONSHIPS	1969

PLAYING RECORD	W	L	T	PCT
AFL Regular Season	87	48	5	.639
NFL Regular Season	190	195	7	.494
AFL Playoffs (4 Appearances)	5	2	0	.714
NFL Playoffs (8 Appearances)	3	8	0	.273

Hunt in 1960 as the Dallas Texans, won their first title in 1962, the year before they moved to Kansas City. By 1970, Dawson and company ranked among the finest teams ever assembled. But a 1971 AFC Western Division title was followed by a stunning Christmas Day overtime playoff loss to Miami that engulfed the franchise in a dark, almost two-decade long haze of futility.

When it ended, Schottenheimer was at the controls and championship talk reached fever pitch at Arrowhead Stadium. He began constructing a big-play defense through the draft (Smith, Thomas, Carter) and introduced a power running attack featuring Okoye and Barry Word. But when it became obvious the Chiefs could not get to a Super Bowl without more offensive spark, he turned to the West Coast offense and brought in an aging Joe Montana to run the show.

Montana, who had directed the 49ers to four Super Bowl titles, took the Chiefs to within a game of the Super Bowl in 1993. But he retired a year later and turned matters over to untested veteran Bono. In what appeared to be a transitional season, Bono and the Chiefs recorded an NFL-best 13 victories before suffering a heart-breaking playoff loss to Indianapolis.

Sack master: Hard-rushing Neil Smith, who led the NFL with 15 sacks in 1993, is a key member of Kansas City's aggressive, turnover-creating defense.

Miami Dolphins

THEY, TOO, WILL PASS

★★★★★★★★★★★

When George Wilson passed the baton of a 4-year-old expansion franchise to new Coach Don Shula in 1970, nobody could have imagined the success story that was about to unfold. But Shula, who had spent the previous seven seasons as coach of the Baltimore Colts, did provide several clues: His first Dolphins team won 10 games and his next three went to the Super Bowl, winning twice. The 1972 Dolphins recorded the only perfect record in NFL history.

By the time the Dolphins had completed that three-year cruise, it was painfully apparent to the rest of the league that Miami under Shula would be no ordinary franchise. Shula supported that theory with consistency and versatility.

His 1971, 1972 and 1973 winners were constructed around a ball-control offense featuring quarterback Bob Griese, running backs Larry Csonka, Jim Kiick and Mercury Morris, wide receiver Paul Warfield and guard Larry Little. The defense included such big-play bashers as linebacker Nick Buoniconti and safeties Jake Scott and Dick Anderson. But Shula's coaching genius was best demonstrated by his ability to convert that controlled running attack of the 1970s to a wide-open passing offense in the 1980s.

The Dolphins played in their fourth Super Bowl after the strike-shortened 1982 season with a journeyman quarterback named David Woodley. But the team's personality changed drastically when strong-armed Dan Marino was drafted in 1983. Shula made a full commitment to the passing attack with the acquisition of deep threats Mark Clayton and Mark Duper. He also beefed up the offensive line to protect his valuable quarterback.

Marino and Shula proved to be a lethal combination. Over 13 seasons, Marino has passed for an NFL-record 48,841 yards and 352 touchdowns while leading the Dolphins to five Eastern Division titles and one Super Bowl appearance—a loss to San Francisco after the 1984 season. The Dolphins have posted only one losing record since Marino's arrival.

Over his 25 Miami seasons before retiring after the 1995 campaign, Shula won 274 games (including playoffs), and his overall total of 347 victories is the all-time record for NFL coaches. The Dolphins, a 9-7 disappointment in Shula's final season, will be passed into the capable hands of Jimmy Johnson, who led Dallas to consecutive Super Bowl victories after the 1992 and 1993 seasons.

Johnson takes over a team in transition. Barring a Marino miracle, the Dolphins, even with running backs Terry Kirby and Bernie Parmalee, guard Keith Sims, and tackle Richmond Webb, could struggle for consistency.

FACTS AND FIGURES

CONFERENCE/DIVISION	AFC East
FIRST YEAR IN NFL	1970 (AFL 1966-69)
STADIUM/CAPACITY/SURFACE	Joe Robbie Stadium (74,916) /Grass
FORMER CITIES/NICKNAMES	None
AFL CHAMPIONSHIPS	None
SUPER BOWL CHAMPIONSHIPS	1972, 1973

PLAYING RECORD	W	L	T	PCT
AFL Regular Season	15	39	2	.286
NFL Regular Season	257	133	2	.658
AFL Playoffs	0	0	0	.000
NFL Playoffs (16 Appearances)	17	14	0	.548

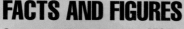

Running commentary: Terry Kirby and other Miami running backs should get more action under new coach Jimmy Johnson.

New England Patriots

BEST-LAID PLANS GO AWRY

How do you give a struggling franchise purpose and direction? How do you turn years of underachieving frustration into consistency and success? Bill Parcells thought he had answered those questions in a surprising 1994 season that left Patriots fans totally unprepared for a 1995 disappointment.

Perhaps the fans should have been prepared, especially those who had survived more than three decades with little to show for their loyalty.

Born in 1960 as the Boston Patriots in the old American Football League, the team was integrated into the NFL in 1970, changed its name to "New England" a year later and struggled through 14 seasons with three one-game playoff appearances to show for its efforts. Over the team's first 34 seasons, it qualified for the playoffs only six times and won a total of four playoff games.

Three came in a dramatic 1985 postseason, when Raymond Berry's Patriots entered the playoffs as a wild-card team and advanced all the way to Super Bowl XX, where they were pounded by the powerful Chicago Bears, 46-10. The Patriots rode Tony Eason's passing to an Eastern Division title in 1986, but a first-round playoff loss to Denver signaled the beginning of a seven-year postseason drought.

Parcells, a two-time Super Bowl winner as coach of the New York Giants, ended that frustration with an exciting, high-scoring 1994 team that posted a 10-6 record and brought new hope to New England. Despite a first-round playoff loss, everything seemed to be in place: the perfect coach, an exciting quarterback and an aggressive, improving defense.

Young Drew Bledsoe was coming off a 1994 season in which he passed for 4,555 yards and 25 touchdowns, and tight end Ben Coates, his favorite target, was coming off an 1,174-yard receiving effort. The young defense appeared to be confident and ready to take the next step forward.

Exactly what happened in 1995 is hard to explain. Bledsoe's numbers dropped to 3,507 yards and 13 touchdowns and he threw 16 interceptions as the AFC's lowest-rated passer. Coates' numbers also dropped, the defense couldn't stop anybody and the once optimistic Patriots dropped to 6-10. The only bright spot was the performance of rookie running back Curtis Martin, who rushed for an AFC-leading 1,487 yards and scored 15 touchdowns.

Parcells' next challenge will be to identify the real Patriots: the 10-6 contenders of 1994 or the 6-10 pretenders of 1995.

Master of all he surveys: Patriots quarterback Drew Bledsoe was brilliant in 1994, but his 1995 performance fell off.

FACTS AND FIGURES

CONFERENCE/DIVISION	AFC East
FIRST YEAR IN NFL	1970 (AFL 1960-69)
STADIUM/CAPACITY/SURFACE	Foxboro Stadium (60,290) /Grass
FORMER CITIES/NICKNAMES	Boston Patriots (1960-70)
AFL CHAMPIONSHIPS	None
SUPER BOWL CHAMPIONSHIPS	None

PLAYING RECORD	W	L	T	PCT
AFL Regular Season	63	68	9	.482
NFL Regular Season	174	218	0	.444
AFL Playoffs (1 Appearance)	1	1	0	.000
NFL Playoffs (6 Appearances)	3	6	0	.400

New York Jets

BREAKING WITH TRADITION

It's easy to understand why the memory of Super Bowl III remains so prominent in Jets lore. It was one of the major upsets in sports history and it was the only championship in the franchise's 36-year existence.

It also was the signature performance for Broadway Joe Namath, the best quarterback in Jets history and one of the most colorful figures the game has ever known. Stupefying oddsmakers who were listing the powerful Baltimore Colts as prohibitive 18-point favorites, Namath made a shocking guarantee that the Jets would win, delivered a 16-7 victory and gave the fledgling American Football League some much-needed respect.

Namath, contrary to exaggerated accounts, did not do it alone. He was surrounded by a talented offensive cast that included running backs Matt Snell and Emerson Boozer and wide receivers George Sauer and Don Maynard. Snell punched through the Colts' defense for 121 yards and Sauer caught eight Namath passes for 133 yards. Weeb Ewbank, who also guided the Baltimore Colts to NFL titles in 1958 and 1959, was the coach.

Riding the crest of that victory, Namath directed the Jets to the 1969 Eastern Division championship. Little did anyone suspect that a 13-6 loss to Kansas City in the AFL playoffs would trigger an 11-year playoff drought during which the Jets would not even post a winning record.

FACTS AND FIGURES

CONFERENCE/DIVISION	AFC East
FIRST YEAR IN NFL	1970 (AFL 1960-69)
STADIUM/CAPACITY/SURFACE	Giants Stadium (77,121) /Artificial
FORMER CITIES/NICKNAMES	New York Titans (1960-62)
AFL CHAMPIONSHIPS	1968
SUPER BOWL CHAMPIONSHIPS	1968

PLAYING RECORD	W	L	T	PCT
AFL Regular Season	69	65	6	.514
NFL Regular Season	161	229	2	.413
AFL Playoffs (2 Appearances)	2	1	0	.666
NFL Playoffs (5 Appearances)	3	5	0	.375

Namath and his chronically sore knees were gone by 1977, as were Snell, Boozer, Sauer and Maynard. The Jets, powered by quarterback Richard Todd, running back Freeman McNeil and wide receiver Wesley Walker, regained their winning ways in 1981 with a 10-5-1 record and almost got back to the Super Bowl a year later when they advanced to the AFC Championship Game before losing a muddy 14-0 battle to Miami.

The Jets would make another playoff push in 1985 and 1986 with Ken O'Brien handing off to McNeil and passing deep to Al Toon. But both seasons ended with playoff losses, as did a 1991 season in which the Jets qualified for postseason play with an 8-8 record.

From 1990-94 under coaches Bruce Coslet and Pete Carroll, the Jets barely kept their heads above water. Former Eagles head Rich Kotite took the reins in 1995 and began reconstructing an ineffective offense after watching his first team struggle to an NFL-worst 3-13 record. He improved the defense, one that featured end Hugh Douglas, linebacker Marvin Jones and cornerback Aaron Glenn, and the picture changed dramatically before the 1996 season when the offense was restructured around free-agent quarterback Neil O'Donnell and big-play receiver Keyshawn Johnson, the draft's No. 1 overall pick.

End result: Young end Hugh Douglas is part of an improving Jets defensive unit.

Oakland Raiders

SILVER AND BLACK AND BLUE

★★★★★★★★★★★

What goes around comes around. That adage has special meaning for Oakland football fans, who are enjoying their second love affair with Al Davis and his itinerant Raiders. When the 1995 Raiders returned to the city where they got their start in 1960 as an American Football League charter member, they punctuated a two-city, controversy-filled existence that has produced an impressive success ledger and a personality that matches their owner's.

Davis has never been afraid to be different and he seems to relish his reputation as a maverick. He has signed reputed "troublemakers" when other teams refused to take a chance; his teams, particularly his defenses, have always been aggressive; and his players revel in the Silver-and-Black mystique.

FACTS AND FIGURES

CONFERENCE/DIVISION	AFC West
FIRST YEAR IN NFL	1970 (AFL 1960-69)
STADIUM/CAPACITY/SURFACE	Oakland Coliseum (54,800) /Grass
FORMER CITIES/NICKNAMES	Oakland Raiders (1960-81); Los Angeles Raiders (1982-94)
AFL CHAMPIONSHIPS	1967
SUPER BOWL CHAMPIONSHIPS	1976, 1980, 1983

PLAYING RECORD	W	L	T	PCT
AFL Regular Season	77	58	5	.568
NFL Regular Season	244	142	6	.630
AFL Playoffs (3 Appearances)	3	3	0	.500
NFL Playoffs (15 Appearances)	18	12	0	.600

Catching on: Sure-handed Tim Brown is the big-play receiver for an Oakland passing game that struggled in 1995.

But his most controversial performance was staged in the courtroom after the NFL denied him permission to move his Raiders from Oakland to Los Angeles in 1980. The Raiders joined the Los Angeles Coliseum Commission in an antitrust suit against the NFL and the long, bitter dispute dragged through the court system for two years before Davis was granted permission to move. The 1995 return was not nearly so painful.

Through all of the controversy, the Raiders have been one of the game's most consistent franchises. Since 1967, when they won their first AFL championship and lost to Green Bay in Super Bowl II, the Raiders have not had more than a four-year playoff drought. That loss to the Packers was the Raiders' only misstep in four Super Bowl appearances. They won after the 1976 season under Coach John Madden, and after the 1980 and 1983 seasons under Tom Flores. Their all-time roster reads like a who's who of football.

Quarterbacks Daryle Lamonica, Ken Stabler, and Jim Plunkett. Running backs Clem Daniels, Mark van Eeghen, and Marcus Allen. Receivers Cliff Branch, Fred Biletnikoff, and Tim Brown, tight ends Dave Casper and Todd Christensen. And defenders like linemen Howie Long and John Matuszak, linebacker Ted Hendricks, cornerbacks Willie Brown and Mike Haynes and safety Jack Tatum.

After that four-year drought under Flores and Mike Shanahan from 1986-89, Art Shell coached the Raiders to three playoff appearances in five years before giving way to Mike White after the 1994 season. White discarded Davis' long-successful "vertical" passing attack and installed a West Coast offense that featured quarterback Jeff Hostetler, big-play receiver Brown and 1,000-yard rusher Harvey Williams.

But the talented Raiders, who were expected to make a 1995 run at the Super Bowl, were an 8-8 disappointment in their Oakland homecoming. A disappointment that won't be tolerated by Davis or Oakland fans with long memories.

Pittsburgh Steelers

ALMOST LIKE OLD TIMES

As all the hoopla surrounding Super Bowl XXX unfolded, it must have seemed like old times to Steelers fans. Quarterback Neil O'Donnell wasn't exactly Terry Bradshaw and the defense wasn't exactly Steel Curtain-caliber, but a Super Bowl is a Super Bowl.

It didn't seem like old times, however, when the Steelers lost to the Dallas Cowboys—the team's first Super Bowl loss in five

Man of Steel: Cornerback Rod Woodson, who doubles as a kick returner, is one of the NFL's most talented cover men and hardest hitters.

appearances. In retrospect for Pittsburgh fans, it was just nice to be there, but old habits die hard.

Winning wasn't always a habit for this franchise. Cigar-chomping Art Rooney brought his Pittsburgh Pirates into the NFL fold in 1933, but it took 40 seasons for the Steelers (renamed in 1941) to win their first division title and 42 seasons for Rooney to realize his dream of an NFL championship.

But the magical 1970s made the wait worthwhile. By the end of the decade, the NFL's most beleaguered franchise had changed into its most glamorous. The transformation took place under Coach Chuck Noll, whose Steelers struggled to a 1-13 first-year record in 1969 but improved to 5-9 and 6-8 as a championship contender took shape.

Building through the draft, Noll fashioned his defense around linemen Mean Joe Greene and LC Greenwood, linebackers Jack Lambert and Jack Ham and cornerback Mel Blount. The offense was constructed around Bradshaw, running back Franco Harris, and wide receivers Lynn Swann and John Stallworth.

When the young Steelers finally won their first Central Division title in 1972, they advanced to the AFC Championship Game. When they reached their first Super Bowl two years later, they defeated Minnesota, 16-6, fulfilling Rooney's dream. The Steelers won a second Super Bowl after the 1975 season and claimed two more after the 1978 and 1979 campaigns. The team that had needed 42 seasons to win a championship was the NFL's first four-time Super Bowl winner.

Noll's coaching reign would last 12 more seasons and produce four playoff appearances—but no more Super Bowls. His replacement, Bill Cowher, quickly re-energized the franchise.

With a ball-control offense featuring power runner Barry Foster and the consistent O'Donnell and a big-play defense featuring linebacker Greg Lloyd and cornerback Rod Woodson, Cowher's 1992 team won the AFC Central Division title, followed with another playoff appearance and advanced to the 1994 AFC Championship Game. The 1995 Steelers, featuring wide receiver Yancey Thigpen in a new passing offense, took that scenario one step beyond.

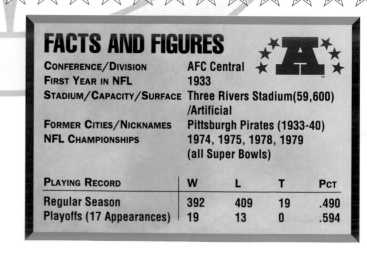

FACTS AND FIGURES

CONFERENCE/DIVISION	AFC Central
FIRST YEAR IN NFL	1933
STADIUM/CAPACITY/SURFACE	Three Rivers Stadium(59,600)/Artificial
FORMER CITIES/NICKNAMES	Pittsburgh Pirates (1933-40)
NFL CHAMPIONSHIPS	1974, 1975, 1978, 1979 (all Super Bowls)

PLAYING RECORD	W	L	T	PCT
Regular Season	392	409	19	.490
Playoffs (17 Appearances)	19	13	0	.594

San Diego Chargers

SEARCHING FOR CONSISTENCY

It must strike long-time Chargers fans as ironic that their 1994 team, with an offense and defense that ranked near the middle of the NFL, would reach the Super Bowl, an accomplishment unmatched by the high-scoring Don Coryell teams from 1979-82. But there they were, facing off in Super Bowl XXIX against a San Francisco team that bore a striking resemblance to the Air-Coryell offensive powers of yesteryear.

 Leading the charge: San Diego quarterback Stan Humphries overcame a number of injuries in 1994 and took his team to Super Bowl XXIX.

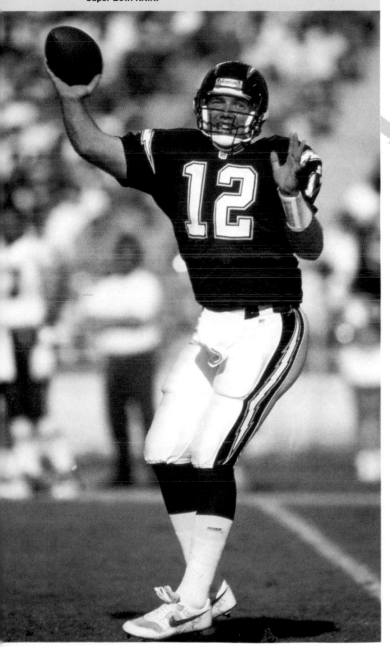

FACTS AND FIGURES

CONFERENCE/DIVISION	AFC West
FIRST YEAR IN NFL	1970 (AFL 1960-69)
STADIUM/CAPACITY/SURFACE	Jack Murphy Stadium (60,789) /Grass
FORMER CITIES/NICKNAMES	Los Angeles Chargers (1960)
AFL CHAMPIONSHIPS	1963
SUPER BOWL CHAMPIONSHIPS	None

PLAYING RECORD	W	L	T	PCT
AFL Regular Season	86	48	6	.636
NFL Regular Season	179	208	5	.463
AFL Playoffs (5 Appearances)	1	4	0	.200
NFL Playoffs (7 Appearances)	6	7	0	.462

But the 49ers who beat the 1994 Chargers, 49-26, had a side to them that the Air-Coryell Chargers did not have—a defensive side. The Air-Coryell Chargers were pure offense, equally capable of scoring and allowing points in bunches.

There's no arguing that was a colorful and exciting period in San Diego football history. Dan Fouts was a prolific passer who delivered the ball to an equally prolific receiving corps that featured tight end Kellen Winslow and wideouts Charlie Joiner, Wes Chandler, and John Jefferson. Chuck Muncie was a dangerous running back, whether carrying the ball or catching it out of the backfield.

But offense alone doesn't win championships and Coryell's Chargers couldn't quite get over the final hurdle. They won three consecutive AFC Western Division titles and reached the AFC Championship Game in back-to-back years, losing to Oakland and Cincinnati after the 1980 and 1981 seasons. Coryell would be gone five years later and the Chargers would reach the playoffs only two more times before Bobby Ross directed them to their surprising 1994 run.

That roller-coaster ride was similar to the one Chargers fans experienced in the early existence of a franchise that began play as the Los Angeles entry of the old American Football League. The Sid Gillman-coached Chargers, who transferred to San Diego after one season, played in five of the first six AFL Championship Games, winning their only title in 1963. After losing in the 1965 title game, the Chargers did not qualify for another playoff until 1979, Coryell's second season as coach.

Ross, aware of that up-and-down history, is trying to settle his Chargers into a pattern of consistency. With a solid but unspectacular offense anchored by quarterback Stan Humphries and wide receiver Tony Martin and a defense featuring linebacker Junior Seau, San Diego took a step in that direction by earning a 1995 wild-card playoff berth, only to fall in the first round to an inspired Colts team.

Sometimes the road to consistency is traveled with slow steps.

Seattle Seahawks

A MATTER OF RESPECT

They have never won a Super Bowl or an AFC championship. They have captured just one division title. And they have qualified for postseason play only four times in 20 years. But that doesn't dim the optimism of Seahawks players and coaches.

Most of that optimism generates from a second-year head coach, a young, talent-laden roster and a 1995 season that provided a light at the end of the tunnel. When Dennis Erickson took the Seattle coaching reins before the 1995 campaign, the team was staring back at a four-year losing streak, six years without a playoff berth and a listless past.

But Erickson appears capable of changing all that. After starting slowly, his first team finished fast and entered the final week with a chance to make the playoffs. A 26-3 loss to AFC West champion Kansas City dispelled that notion, but a final 8-8 record and a solid player nucleus suggest a bright future.

Erickson's hopes center around quarterback Rick Mirer, who was drafted in 1993, and Chris Warren, who has strung together four consecutive 1,000-yard rushing seasons. With Mirer throwing to Brian Blades and Joey Galloway and Warren running behind tackle Howard Ballard, the offense is well fortified. Cortez Kennedy is a highlight-film tackle for a defense that still needs help at several key positions. It all adds up to an improving team that could make fans forget about past transgressions.

But the Seahawks have had their moments. Born in 1976 in an NFL expansion that also included Tampa Bay, Seattle struggled to a 2-12 season under Coach Jack Patera. The young Seahawks, with quarterback Jim Zorn firing to receiver Steve Largent, surprised the football world two years later with a 9-7 record and proved that was no fluke by matching the mark in 1979.

The best came in 1983, Chuck Knox's first season as coach. The Seahawks finished 9-7, tied for second in the AFC West and earned their first playoff berth. In an unlikely run that came up just short of the Super Bowl, Seattle knocked off Denver and Miami before falling to the LA Raiders, 30-14, in the AFC Championship Game.

The Seahawks, featuring the passing of Dave Krieg to Largent and the 1,000-yard rushing of Curt Warner, finished 12-4 the next season and won another playoff game before falling in the divisional round to Miami. They would appear in two more playoffs and win their first AFC West title in 1988 before starting their current seven-year postseason drought.

Sleepless in Seattle: Rick Mirer, the Seahawks' talented young quarterback, hopes to awaken a long-dormant franchise.

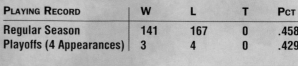

FACTS AND FIGURES

CONFERENCE/DIVISION	AFC West	
FIRST YEAR IN NFL	1976	
STADIUM/CAPACITY/SURFACE	Kingdome (66,400)/Artificial	
FORMER CITIES/NICKNAMES	None	
SUPER BOWL CHAMPIONSHIPS	None	

PLAYING RECORD	W	L	T	PCT
Regular Season	141	167	0	.458
Playoffs (4 Appearances)	3	4	0	.429

Arizona Cardinals

NOWHERE TO GO BUT UP

Success never has come easily for the Cardinals. From their early days in Chicago to their second and third lives in St. Louis and Phoenix, progress has been tedious at best. In 40 Chicago seasons, the Cardinals won two NFL championships and made three postseason appearances. It took 14 seasons for the St. Louis Cardinals to capture an NFC Eastern Division title and make their postseason debut. The Arizona Cardinals still are looking for their first winning record after eight seasons in Phoenix.

They inched closer in 1994 when they posted an 8-8 mark under new Coach Buddy Ryan, whose take-no-prisoners style and guarantees of success re-energized impatient fans. But they slid back into the NFC East basement in 1995 as Ryan's team slumped to a four-12 record which lead to the hiring of Colts' defensive co-ordinator, Vince Tobin, as new coach.

Tobin will try to rebuild the team—and bring the city its first playoff berth. That would be welcome tonic for fans who embraced Bill Bidwill and his Cardinals when they made the move from St. Louis in 1988. To pull off that trick, Tobin will need to patch some significant defensive holes, find a young quarterback and coax big seasons out of running backs Garrison Hearst and Larry Centers and wide receiver Rob Moore.

The Cardinals are the oldest continuously-run pro football franchise, founded in 1898 and joining the NFL as a charter member in 1920. The Cardinals of the 1920s and 1930s featured such players as halfback-quarterback Paddy Driscoll, end Guy Chamberlin, and fullback Ernie Nevers. The 1947 and 1948 Cardinals, who appeared in consecutive NFL Championship Games and won the organization's second title (1947), were fueled by the running of Charley Trippi and Elmer Angsman.

But the most exciting team in St. Louis history was created in the mid-1970s by offensive genius Don Coryell. The explosive Cardinals, with Jim Hart throwing to such receivers as Mel Gray, Ike Harris and Jackie Smith and handing off to Terry Metcalf and Jim Otis, rolled up points and won consecutive division titles (1974 and 1975), only to lose in the first round of the playoffs both years. The Cardinals' only other brush with success came in the strike-shortened 1982 season when five-time 1,000-yard rusher Ottis Anderson led Jim Hanifan's team into the playoffs. But once again the season came to a halt with a first-round loss to (Green Bay).

Flying High: Arizona wide receiver Rob Moore (top) is one of the stars the Cardinals are looking to as they rebuild under new coach Vince Tobin.

FACTS AND FIGURES

CONFERENCE/DIVISION	NFC East
FIRST YEAR IN NFL	1920
STADIUM/CAPACITY/SURFACE	Sun Devil Stadium (73,521)/Grass
FORMER CITIES/NICKNAMES	Chicago Cardinals (1920-59); St. Louis Cardinals (1960-87); Phoenix Cardinals (1988-93)
NFL CHAMPIONSHIPS	1925, 1947
SUPER BOWL CHAMPIONSHIPS	None

PLAYING RECORD	W	L	T	PCT
Regular Season	395	544	39	.423
Playoffs (5 Appearances)	1	4	0	.200

Atlanta Falcons

SEARCHING FOR THE MISSING LINK

I n their 30-year existence, the Atlanta Falcons have tried everything. They have sampled life as a running team, they have speeded up their attack with a passing blitz and they have tried mixing their offensive weapons. So far, the results have been unspectacular.

The Falcons have qualified for postseason play only five times and they have only two playoff victories to show for three decades. Three of the appearances came under Leeman Bennett in 1978, 1980 and 1982; the fourth came in 1991 under Jerry Glanville, and the fifth in 1995 under June Jones. Only two other Atlanta teams have posted winning records.

That's not to say the Falcons haven't been exciting. They have had six 1,000-yard rushers (Dave Hampton, William Andrews, Gerald Riggs, John Settle, Erric Pegram, and Craig Heyward), eight 1,000-yard receivers (Wallace Francis, Alfred Jenkins, Stacey Bailey, Andre Rison, Michael Haynes, Terance Mathis, Eric Metcalf, and Bert Emanuel) and two of the great kick returners in NFL history (Billy White Shoes Johnson and Deion Sanders). Quarterback Steve Bartkowski passed for 23,468 yards over 11 Atlanta seasons.

But something always seems to be missing. Often it's defense.

Armed and dangerous: Quarterback Jeff George, the first overall pick of the 1990 draft, has found life away from Indianapolis more to his liking.

FACTS AND FIGURES

CONFERENCE/DIVISION	NFC West	
FIRST YEAR IN NFL	1966	
STADIUM/CAPACITY/SURFACE	Georgia Dome (71,280) /Artificial	
FORMER CITIES/NICKNAMES	None	
NFL CHAMPIONSHIPS	None	
SUPER BOWL CHAMPIONSHIPS	None	

PLAYING RECORD	W	L	T	PCT
Regular Season	172	271	5	.390
Playoffs (5 Appearances)	2	5	0	.286

Sometimes it's clutch offensive play. Always it's the ability to combine the two in that one championship push.

The Falcons were born as an expansion team in 1966, the year the AFL-NFL merger was announced. When the team struggled to post six total victories over the first three seasons under first-time coach Norb Hecker, the former Green Bay assistant was replaced by Norm Van Brocklin. The Falcons improved to 6-8 the next season (1969) and posted Atlanta's first winning record (7-6-1) in 1971.

But it wasn't until Bennett took over in 1977 that a brighter future appeared realistic. With Bartkowski leading the charge, the Falcons reached the playoffs three times in six years, posted their first postseason victory (1978) and captured their first division title (1980). But that run was Atlanta's last hurrah until 1991, when Chris Miller directed the Falcons to a 10-6 record and a first-round playoff victory using Glanville's "Red Gun" offense.

But again the Falcons failed to sustain their momentum. After consecutive 6-10 seasons, Glanville gave way to Jones and Miller was replaced by Jeff George. With George firing to Mathis, Emanuel and Metcalf and handing off to Heyward, the 1995 Falcons scored lots of points, earned a wild-card playoff berth and were defeated by Green Bay in a first-round loss.

Jones' hopes of reaching loftier heights will depend on his ability to find that missing element—in this case, defense.

Carolina Panthers

EXPANDING HORIZONS

E xpansion life is not recommended for the faint of heart. Right of passage normally requires a little heartache, periods of frustration and plenty of losses. But the 1995 Panthers were living, winning proof that it doesn't have to be that way.

After opening their campaign with an expansion-like five straight losses, the Panthers rallied behind a rookie quarterback (Kerry Collins), a young offensive line and an opportunistic defense to win a first-year-record seven games. They came within three points (a 20-17 season-closing loss to Washington) of a .500 debut, and one of their victories was the defending Super Bowl-champion San Francisco 49ers.

En route to their 7-9 finish and surprising challenge for an NFC wild-

FACTS AND FIGURES

CONFERENCE/DIVISION	NFC West
FIRST YEAR IN NFL	1995
STADIUM/CAPACITY/SURFACE	Carolinas Stadium (72,500) /grass
PLAYING RECORD	7-9, first NFL season

card playoff berth, the Panthers:

Toppled the old expansion mark of three victories, which was also broken by the Jacksonville Jaguars (4-12). Four of Carolina's victories came in succession, another record.

Posted a 5-3 record in home games at Clemson's Memorial Stadium. Including preseason games, the Panthers were 7-3 at home.

Became the third team in history to lose its first five games and win its next four. Three of the Panthers' seven victories were over playoff teams.

This expansion beast was trained and guided by first-year NFL Coach Dom Capers, who built his lineup around talented rookies, waiver-wire pickups and free-agent signees. Collins replaced veteran Frank Reich in the Panthers' fourth game and led them to a 6-6 record as a starter. Fellow rookies Blake Brockermeyer (tackle) and Frank Garcia (guard) anchored an improving offensive line, Willie Green showed signs of becoming a big-play receiver and third-year running back Derrick Moore ran for 740 yards. Veterans Sam Mills (linebacker) and Brett Maxie (safety) keyed a defense that allowed 20.3 points per game.

It was a team that refused to wilt under pressure and one that is positioned to rise quickly into prominence. Capers already has an outstanding mix of rookies and veterans and he can plug holes through the draft and free agency.

Whether the Panthers can live up to the lofty expectations they created for themselves in 1995 remains to be seen. But one thing is sure: They have shown a willingness to spend money and a dedication to winning.

That dedication will be on display in 1996 and beyond at new Carolinas Stadium, a bright new home for a bright new franchise.

On the prowl: The first-year Panthers, under the direction of former Pittsburgh defensive coordinator Dom Capers, surprised the football world with their 7-9 record.

Chicago Bears

A GLORIOUS PAST, BY GEORGE

When George Halas died in 1983, he had been the driving force behind Chicago football for 64 years. He had seen a little of everything in his long-time roles of founder, player, coach, owner and No. 1 fan of football's most celebrated franchise.

The team that was taking shape at the time of Papa Bear's death probably would have triggered fond memories.

The 1985 Bears, who captured Chicago's first Super Bowl and first NFL championship in 22 years, were a throwback to Halas'

Bearing down: Quarterback Erik Kramer threw 29 touchdown passes in 1995 and guided the Bears to within a whisker of another playoff berth.

FACTS AND FIGURES

CONFERENCE/DIVISION	NFC Central
FIRST YEAR IN NFL	1920
STADIUM/CAPACITY/SURFACE	Soldier Field (66,950)/Grass
FORMER CITIES/NICKNAMES	Decatur Staleys (1920); Chicago Staleys (1921)
NFL CHAMPIONSHIPS	1921, 1932, 1933, 1940, 1941, 1943, 1946, 1963, 1985 (Super Bowl)

PLAYING RECORD	W	L	T	PCT
Regular Season	591	385	42	.601
Playoffs (21	14	14	0	.500

1930s "Monsters of the Midway" teams that featured colorful characters and good, old-fashioned power football.

The heart of that team was a ferocious defense that showcased free-spirit linemen Dan Hampton and Steve McMichael, 340-pound rookie tackle William (Refrigerator) Perry and linebacker Mike Singletary, one of the most intense competitors ever to play the game. Running back Walter Payton was nicknamed "Sweetness," quarterback Jim McMahon was a borderline punk rocker and ever-intense Coach Mike Ditka was an emotional motivator.

What the team lacked in finesse, it made up for with victories.

It finished the regular season 15-1, shut out the Giants and Rams in playoff games and overpowered New England in Super Bowl XX, 46-10. The Bears went on to win NFC Central Division titles in four of the next five years, but failed to return to another Super Bowl.

It was easy to understand why these Bears resembled the Bears of old. Ditka was a former player under Halas and was hired by Papa Bear to turn around a long championship drought. There hadn't been many droughts in Halas' 40-year coaching career, which was served in four 10-year shifts. Halas, one of the league's founding fathers in 1920 when the Bears broke in as the Decatur Staleys, watched his teams win eight NFL championships—more than any team except the Packers.

He also coached such Hall of Fame-bound players as Doug Atkins, Dick Butkus, Bill George, Red Grange, Bill Hewitt, Sid Luckman, George Musso, Bronko Nagurski, Gale Sayers, Joe Stydahar and George Trafton.

When Ditka's successful 11-year coaching regime ended with a 5-11 record in 1992, the Bears hired Cowboys defensive coordinator Dave Wannstedt, who has built a strong offense around quarterback Erik Kramer, running back Rashaan Salaam and wide receiver Curtis Conway. The 1994 Bears qualified for the playoffs and the 1995 team just missed.

Dallas Cowboys

A MODEL OF CONSISTENCY

Love 'em or hate 'em, there's no denying the Cowboys are the premier franchise in professional football. Consider: Since the team entered the NFL in 1960, it has posted only 10 losing records — half coming in its first five seasons.

The team has had three coaches and one location in 36 years. From 1966 through 1985, the Cowboys strung together an NFL-record 20 consecutive winning seasons and qualified for the playoffs in 18 of them.

The Cowboys have played in eight Super Bowls, winning a record-tying five times. The latest, a Super Bowl XXX victory over Pittsburgh, was their third in four years. That success is not a mystery. From the moment of their birth, the Cowboys have been blessed with great management, coaching and, soon after, great players. Tex Schramm and stone-faced Coach Tom Landry (under original owner Clint Murchison Jr., and his successor HR (Bum) Bright) built the Cowboys into "America's Team" from 1960. A new owner Jerry Jones, who bought the team in 1989, added to the success story with the help of coaches Jimmy Johnson and Barry Switzer.

Five of the Dallas Super Bowl appearances came in a nine-year stretch from 1970-78 under Landry, who turned over his offense to Roger Staubach, a former Heisman Trophy-winning quarterback from Navy. Joining Staubach in Dallas' big-play attack were such running backs as Duane Thomas, Robert Newhouse and Tony Dorsett and such receivers as Drew Pearson, Golden Richards and Tony Hill. Defensively, the Cowboys were blessed with the likes of Bob Lilly, Lee Roy Jordan, Harvey Martin, Randy White, Ed (Too Tall) Jones, Cliff Harris and Charlie Waters.

When the decade turned, the Cowboys continued winning—but there would be no more Super Bowls until 1992. Landry gave way to Johnson after the 1988 season—his 29th as the only coach in Dallas history—and Johnson led the team out of a five-year funk that included a 1-15 record in 1989.

With the triple-threat combination of quarterback Troy Aikman, running back Emmitt Smith and wide receiver Michael Irvin and a stout, mistake-forcing defense, the 1992 Cowboys stormed to a 13-3 record, swept through the playoffs and pounded Buffalo, 52-17, in Super Bowl XXVII. They followed with a 30-13 Super Bowl victory over the Bills a year later. When Johnson left after a disagreement with Jones, Switzer led the 1995 Cowboys to a Super Bowl victory over Pittsburgh. Free-agency defections have taken a toll, but the Aikman-Smith-Irvin combination remains intact and the Cowboys appear capable of challenging for NFL supremacy deep into the 1990s.

Sooner or later: Former Oklahoma and UCLA quarterback Troy Aikman is the one of the NFL's brightest stars, leading Dallas to three Super Bowl victories.

FACTS AND FIGURES

CONFERENCE/DIVISION	NFC East
FIRST YEAR IN NFL	1960
STADIUM/CAPACITY/SURFACE	Texas Stadium (65,024) /Artificial
FORMER CITIES/NICKNAMES	None
SUPER BOWL CHAMPIONSHIPS	1971, 1977, 1992, 1993, 1995 (all Super Bowl)

PLAYING RECORD	W	L	T	PCT
Regular Season	318	206	6	.606
Playoffs (23 Appearances)	31	18	0	.633

Detroit Lions

A BREATH OF FRESH AIR

In the six-plus decades of Detroit's NFL membership, nobody had seen anything like Barry Sanders. He arrived in 1989 after a Heisman Trophy-winning season at Oklahoma State, juked and nuked his way to 1,470 rookie yards and made it clear he would be an NFL force for years to come. Sanders was the answer to more than a few prayers.

Before his arrival, the Lions had not appeared in a postseason game since 1983 and had only three playoff appearances to show for 31 years. After winning three NFL championships and another Western Conference crown from 1952-57, the Lions had stagnated for three decades without the players or the game plan to get back on top.

But Sanders provided an instant game plan. The Lions and Coach Wayne Fontes began filling in pieces around their star, beefing up the offensive line and drafting go-to wide receiver Herman Moore with a 1991 first-round draft pick.

With Rodney Peete, Andre Ware and Erik Kramer shuffling in and out of the quarterback job, the Lions roared to a 12-4 record in 1991 and claimed the NFC Central Division title. A divisional playoff victory over Dallas vaulted them into the NFC title game, where they lost to Washington. They captured another division title in 1993 and reached the playoffs in 1994 and 1995.

Sanders completed the 1994 season with 1,883 rushing yards and 1995 with 1,500—his fixth and seventh consecutive 1,000-yard efforts. And by the end of the 1995 campaign, the Lions' offense, now being directed by quarterback Scott Mitchell, was being hailed as a big-time point producer. The combination of Sanders, Mitchell and wideouts Moore and Brett Perriman with an improving defense bodes well for a franchise that has not always had reason for optimism.

Born in 1930 as the Portsmouth Spartans, the team moved to Detroit in 1934, won its first championship in 1935 and wasn't heard from again until its 1950s run. That outstanding stretch was orchestrated by such offensive stars as quarterback Bobby Layne, halfback Doak Walker and end Leon Hart and a defense built around linebacker Joe Schmidt and cornerback Yale Lary.

Twenty-five years after their last championship in 1957, four-time 1,000-yard rusher Billy Sims led a charge that produced a division title and consecutive playoff appearances in 1982 and 1983.

FACTS AND FIGURES

CONFERENCE/DIVISION	NFC Central
FIRST YEAR IN NFL	1930
STADIUM/CAPACITY/SURFACE	Pontiac Silverdome (80,365)/Artificial
FORMER CITIES/NICKNAMES	Portsmouth Spartans (1930-33)
NFL CHAMPIONSHIPS	1935, 1952, 1953, 1957
SUPER BOWL CHAMPIONSHIPS	None

PLAYING RECORD	W	L	T	PCT
Regular Season	421	428	32	.496
Playoffs (12 Appearances)	7	8	0	.467

 20-20 vision: Lions running back Barry Sanders has posted seven straight 1,000-yard seasons.

Green Bay Packers

THE LONG ROAD BACK

The cry has been heard off and on for 27 years: "The Pack is back." But "back" is a long way for this team and the onus of past success will never make life easy for players and fans in the NFL's smallest city.

Like when Coach Mike Holmgren and quarterback Brett Favre led the Packers into the 1993, 1994 and 1995 playoffs, only the team's third, fourth and fifth postseason appearances in 28 years. Despite their success, including an 11-5 record in 1995, people talked about the team's long title drought. That happens when you're spoiled.

Many NFL fans regard the Packers' extended period of futility as

The Pack is back: 1995 MVP Brett Favre has Packers fans thinking about a return to championship form.

FACTS AND FIGURES

CONFERENCE/DIVISION	NFC Central
FIRST YEAR IN NFL	1921
STADIUM/CAPACITY/SURFACE	Lambeau Field (59,543)/Grass
FORMER CITIES/NICKNAMES	None
NFL CHAMPIONSHIPS	1929, 1930, 1931, 1936, 1939, 1944, 1961, 1962, 1965, 1966, 1967
SUPER BOWL CHAMPIONSHIPS	1966, 1967

PLAYING RECORD	W	L	T	PCT
Regular Season	514	434	36	.541
Playoffs (16 Appearances)	17	8	0	.680

fitting payback for the most glorious run in history. They remember the Vince Lombardi machine of the 1960s that mowed down their teams with frightening consistency en route to five NFL championships and victories in the first two Super Bowls.

The Packers of the Lombardi era were molded offensively around quarterback Bart Starr, halfback Paul Hornung, fullback Jim Taylor and receivers Carroll Dale, Marv Fleming and Max McGee. End Willie Davis and tackle Henry Jordan anchored a defense that also included linebacker Ray Nitschke and backs Herb Adderley and Willie Wood.

While that run was the highlight of the franchise's storied history, it wasn't the only one. The Packers, members of the NFL since 1921, won consecutive championships in 1929, 1930 and 1931 under long-time coach and founder Curly Lambeau. That team was built around halfback Johnny (Blood) McNally, tackle Cal Hubbard and guard Mike Michalske. The Packers struck again in 1936, 1939 and 1944 with Arnie Herber and Cecil Isbell throwing to end Don Hutson.

When Lombardi claimed his fifth championship and the franchise's record 11th in Super Bowl II against Oakland, he retired, setting the stage for the Packers' long playoff drought.

There were good players in the 1970s and 1980s: three-time 1,000-yard rusher John Brockington, quarterback Lynn Dickey, wide receiver James Lofton, linebacker Dave Robinson. But not enough to get the team back to the top. The 1995 Packers made a strong title push behind Favre, 1,000-yard rusher Edgar Bennett and wide receiver Robert Brooks, upsetting San Francisco and advancing to the NFC Championship Game. But a defense built around sack master Reggie White could not control Dallas' powerful offense.

If Holmgren can get more defensive help to complement Favre and the high-powered Green Bay offense, the future could produce another title or two. The Pack could indeed be back.

Minnesota Vikings

IMAGES FROZEN IN TIME

The historical images of Vikings football are vivid. Icy turf and snow-covered sidelines. Players blowing into frozen hands and pacing to keep warm. Steam-like breath drifting from faceless helmets. Stone-faced Coach Bud Grant standing stoically near the bench. The Purple People Eaters. Joe Kapp, Fran Tarkenton, Tommy Kramer, Chuck Foreman and Ahmad Rashad.

For a team that didn't even exist until 1961, the Vikings have carved out an impressive history. Four Super Bowl appearances. Two more NFC Championship Games. Eighteen postseason appearances. Two hundred and eighty regular-season victories—an average of eight per season.

That's an amazing run of consistency, especially when you consider the expansion Vikings averaged only 4.6 victories over their first seven years. In their ninth season, the Vikings played in the franchise's first Super Bowl. In their 16th, they played in its fourth—more than any team up to that point.

But despite all those victories, all those Super Bowls, all the great players who have graced the frozen fields of Metropolitan Stadium and the air-conditioned turf of the Metrodome, something is missing from Minnesota's record books. The Vikings have never won Super Bowl.

Quarterback Kapp and a "Purple People Eater" defense featuring linemen Carl Eller, Alan Page and Jim Marshall led Grant's Vikings into Super Bowl IV, where they lost in a shocking upset to AFL champ Kansas City. Four years later, the scrambling Tarkenton and running back Foreman sparked another surge that resulted in three Super Bowl appearances in four years. Minnesota lost to Miami, Pittsburgh and Oakland.

The Vikings have not played in a Super Bowl for 19 years, Grant is long retired after 18 seasons and 168 victories and Metropolitan Stadium and its frigid home-field advantage is a distant memory. But the Vikings remain a consistent winner.

After a brief downturn in the early 1980s, the Vikings surged back and have earned playoff berths in six of the last nine seasons. Three came in a four-year stretch under Coach Dennis Green, who also directed two NFC Central title winners.

Green's future success will depend on his ability to rebuild a sagging defense that has been hit hard by free-agent defections. And he also needs to coax another year or two out of 39-year-old quarterback Warren Moon, who showed in 1995 that he still can deliver the ball to talented receivers Cris Carter and Jake Reed. If the defense rebounds quickly and Moon remains effective, the Vikings could rekindle warm memories of an icy past.

Moon shot: Quarterback Warren Moon led the Vikings to the 1994 NFC Central Division championship, but they fell back to 8-8 in a disappointing 1995 campaign.

FACTS AND FIGURES

CONFERENCE/DIVISION	NFC Central
FIRST YEAR IN NFL	1961
STADIUM/CAPACITY/SURFACE	Metrodome (63,000)/Artificial
FORMER CITIES/NICKNAMES	None
NFL CHAMPIONSHIPS	1969
SUPER BOWL CHAMPIONSHIPS	None

PLAYING RECORD	W	L	T	PCT
Regular Season	280	229	9	.549
Playoffs (18 Appearances)	13	18	0	.419

New Orleans Saints

DEFENSE AND FUNDAMENTALS

No city has felt the growing pains of its infant football team quite like New Orleans. Pain as in futility, disbelief, embarrassment. It got so bad for awhile that Saints fans dubbed themselves the "Aints" and attended games wearing paper bags over their heads—to hide their identity.

Jim Mora changed all that. Mora, a former coach in the United States Football League, took the New Orleans coaching reins in 1986, began preaching the gospel of fundamentals and defense and led the 1987 Saints to their first winning record—ever. After 20 seasons, nine head coaches, 196 losses and 11 last-place finishes in the NFC's Western Division, the Saints posted a 12-3 record (second place behind San Francisco) and made their first postseason appearance, losing to the Minnesota Vikings.

Over the next six seasons, Mora's Saints remained an NFC force. While the division-rival 49ers were piling up points with their "West Coast" offense, New Orleans was pounding out victories with its hard-hitting, big-play defense. The heart of that defense was one of the great linebacking corps in NFL history featuring Rickey Jackson, Sam Mills, Vaughan Johnson and Pat Swilling, all multiple Pro Bowl performers.

Mora's ball-control offense, with quarterback Bobby Hebert handing off to running backs Dalton Hilliard and Rueben Mayes and firing passes to wideout Eric Martin, produced just enough points to keep the Saints in the winning column.

That formula resulted in playoff berths in 1990, 1991 and 1992 and another first—an NFC West championship in 1991. But that 11-5 team, like the two playoff qualifiers before and the one after, fell in the opening round, leaving the Saints winless in the postseason. It also left Mora with the understanding that while defense wins games during the regular season, you also have to be able to score in the playoffs.

Burdened by aging players, inconsistent offense and free-agent defections, Mora saw his Saints slide to 8-8 in 1993 and 7-9 the next two seasons. And with San Francisco riding the crest of a fifth franchise Super Bowl championship and four consecutive NFC West titles, he now faces the difficult task of getting the Saints back to a competitive level.

Mora has an experienced quarterback in Jim Everett, a big-play wide receiver in Michael Haynes and a dependable running back in Mario Bates. But his trademark stingy defense is undergoing reconstructive surgery. Fans are hoping for a short rehabilitation.

FACTS AND FIGURES

CONFERENCE/DIVISION	NFC West
FIRST YEAR IN NFL	1967
STADIUM/CAPACITY/SURFACE	Louisiana Superdome (69,065) /Artificial
FORMER CITIES/NICKNAMES	None
NFL CHAMPIONSHIPS	None
SUPER BOWL CHAMPIONSHIPS	None

PLAYING RECORD	W	L	T	PCT
Regular Season	174	255	5	.407
Playoffs (4 Appearances)	0	4	0	.000

Firing line: Quarterback Jim Everett has brought more firepower to the conservative New Orleans offense.

New York Giants

SEVERAL GIANT STEPS FORWARD

It was a formidable task, the kind of job that can make or break a career. For 19 long years, the once-proud Giants had been suspended in football animation, flustered by inept play, weak drafts and coaching. Bill Parcells was being asked to change all of that.

Big strides: Quarterback Dave Brown is getting passing grades as guiding force for the rebuilding Giants.

FACTS AND FIGURES

CONFERENCE/DIVISION	NFC East		
FIRST YEAR IN NFL	1925		
STADIUM/CAPACITY/SURFACE	Giants Stadium (77,541) /Artificial		
FORMER CITIES/NICKNAMES	None		
NFL CHAMPIONSHIPS	1927, 1934, 1938, 1956, 1986 (Super Bowl), 1990 (Super Bowl)		

PLAYING RECORD	W	L	T	PCT
Regular Season	507	414	32	.549
Playoffs (23 Appearances)	14	18	0	.438

Long-suffering fans were understandably skeptical. The Giants had not enjoyed success since an eight-year period from 1956-63 when they appeared in six NFL Championship Games. Frank Gifford. Sam Huff. Alex Webster. Y.A. Tittle. Rosey Grier. Charlie Conerly. The names mockingly saluted a franchise that remained locked in its past.

Nothing appeared different in 1983 when Parcells' first Giants team struggled to a 3-12-1 record, their 17th non-winning season in 20 years. But the picture suddenly changed when they earned consecutive playoff berths with 9-7 and 10-6 records. The best was yet to come.

The 1986 Giants were a defensive monster featuring linebackers Lawrence Taylor, Carl Banks and Harry Carson and ends George Martin and Leonard Marshall. They ravaged opponents during a 14-2 regular season that produced an NFC Eastern Division title and playoff victories over San Francisco and Washington. Most of the offensive load was carried by Joe Morris, who rushed for 1,516 yards.

But it was quarterback Phil Simms who stole the spotlight in a 39-20 Super Bowl victory over Denver, ravaging the Broncos with 22 completions in 25 attempts for 268 yards and three touchdowns. The Giants had their first NFL championship in 30 years and fifth overall.

The Giants were at it again four years later when they rolled to another division title, playoff victories over Chicago and San Francisco and a 20-19 Super Bowl victory over Buffalo. Taylor, Banks and Marshall again powered the defensive charge, but Jeff Hostetler had replaced the injured Simms and Ottis Anderson earned Super Bowl MVP honors with a 102-yard rushing effort.

Parcells stepped down after that championship and things haven't been the same since. After two disappointing seasons under Ray Handley, former Broncos coach Dan Reeves came in to revive hope with 11-5 and 9-7 records. But the 1995 Giants slipped to 5-11, the defensive monsters turned into pussycats and the offense, retooled around running back Rodney Hampton and young quarterback Dave Brown, struggled to score points.

Reeves' hopes to match Parcells' winning legacy will depend on his ability to reconstruct an aging roster. But thanks to Parcells, at least now there's reason for optimism.

Philadelphia Eagles

A RAY OF HOPE

For most of their first 45 seasons, the Eagles experienced a life of extremes. They won three NFL Championship Games, lost to the Chicago Cardinals in another—and failed to qualify for postseason play 41 times.

That all-or-nothing attitude was instilled by Bert Bell, who brought the former Frankford Yellow Jackets team into the 1933 NFL as the Eagles and coached it from 1936-40 before becoming league

Running Watters: Former 49ers star Ricky Watters has brought respect to the Eagles' running game.

FACTS AND FIGURES

CONFERENCE/DIVISION	NFC East
FIRST YEAR IN NFL	1933
STADIUM/CAPACITY/SURFACE	Veterans Stadium (65,178) /Artificial
FORMER CITIES/NICKNAMES	None
NFL CHAMPIONSHIPS	1948, 1949, 1960
SUPER BOWL CHAMPIONSHIPS	None

PLAYING RECORD	W	L	T	PCT
Regular Season	366	436	23	.458
Playoffs (12 Appearances)	9	10	0	.474

commissioner in 1946. Bell's Eagles accomplished nothing in their first 14 seasons, but they advanced to three straight championship games from 1947-49, winning twice and offering hope for a more lucrative future.

But the success of quarterback Tommy Thompson, running back Steve Van Buren and receiver Pete Pihos were lost in the haze of the next 28 seasons, which produced one playoff berth. The 1960 Eagles, led by aging quarterback Norm Van Brocklin, flanker Tommy McDonald and linebacker Chuck Bednarik, rolled to a 10-2 regular-season record and claimed the franchise's third and final title. It would mark the team's last postseason berth until 1978.

That's when the Eagles began a more conventional existence under Coach Dick Vermeil. With quarterback Ron Jaworski, three-time 1,000-yard rusher Wilbert Montgomery, wide receiver Harold Carmichael and linebacker Bill Bergey, Vermeil's Eagles earned four straight playoff berths and the 1980 team advanced to Super Bowl XV, where it lost to Oakland.

A 1981 wild-card loss signaled the beginning of another six-year playoff drought, but the late 1980s Eagles came to life under Buddy Ryan and later qualified for postseason play in five of eight seasons under Ryan, Rich Kotite, and current coach Ray Rhodes.

Ryan built a defensive monster around all-everything end Reggie White, tackle Jerome Brown, linebackers Seth Joyner and Clyde Simmons and cornerback Eric Allen. Scrambling quarterback Randall Cunningham generated enough offense to make the Eagles a consistent NFC East contender.

Unfortunately for Ryan, the Eagles failed to win a playoff game from 1988-90, costing him his job. Under Kotite, misfortune and free agency took a big toll. Brown died in a tragic automobile accident before the 1992 season and White signed a hefty free-agent contract with Green Bay after it. Simmons and Joyner became free-agent defectors in 1994. Allen left in 1995. Rhodes revived the sagging Eagles in 1995 behind quarterback Rodney Peete, 1,000-yard rusher Ricky Watters and a young, improving defense. Whether Rhodes can continue that upward mobility into the late 1990s remains to be seen.

St. Louis Rams

ANOTHER NEW BEGINNING

From Dan Reeves to Carroll Rosenbloom to Georgia Frontiere, Rams owners have never worried about being different. From Cleveland to Los Angeles to St. Louis, those differences have been manifested in creative and unprecedented ways.

Reeves was the man who stretched the NFL into a coast-to-coast operation when he moved his NFL-champion Rams from Cleveland to Los Angeles in 1946. Rosenbloom was the former Baltimore owner who shocked the football world in 1972 by trading franchises with Robert Irsay—Rosenbloom's Colts for Irsay's Rams. Frontiere, Rosenbloom's widow and the only female owner in NFL history, moved her team to St. Louis before the 1995 season.

On the field, the Rams have been less conspicuous. They have won only two NFL championships but were annual contenders through most of the 1970s and 1980s. The first of those titles came in 1945, the franchise's ninth and final season in Cleveland. The second came in 1951, its sixth season in Los Angeles. The first was orchestrated by Bob Waterfield and the second by Waterfield and Norm Van Brocklin, one of the greatest 1-2 quarterback punches in history.

But life in the late 1950s and 1960s was not so kind. There were only two playoff appearances (under Coach George Allen and quarterback Roman Gabriel) until the 1973 arrival of Coach Chuck Knox, who quickly turned the Rams into a dangerous team. Using a succession of quarterbacks (John Hadl, James Harris, Pat Haden) and four-time 1,000-yard rusher Lawrence McCutcheon, Knox guided the Rams to five straight playoff berths before giving way to Ray Malavasi, who stretched the streak to eight and directed the Rams into their only Super Bowl (1979).

After two down seasons, John Robinson coached the Rams through another run that included playoff appearances in six of seven seasons. Robinson's teams featured Eric Dickerson, who topped 1,000 yards four straight years and rushed for an NFL-record 2,105 in 1984. But the Rams were mired in a string of five consecutive double-digit losing seasons when they began their first year in St. Louis under new Coach Rich Brooks.

Brooks inherited a rebuilding team that celebrated its midwest arrival by winning its first four games and five of its first six. But a potentially big season slipped into a 7-9 disappointment as a young defense collapsed, the running game broke down and quarterback Chris Miller suffered a series of career-threatening concussions.

The season's brightest moments were provided by young wide receiver Isaac Bruce, who caught 119 passes for 1,781 yards and 13 touchdowns. With Bruce doing Jerry Rice-like impersonations, all Brooks needs to figure out is how to get him the ball. Without Miller, who may not play again, that could be a challenge.

Better to receive: Speedy Isaac Bruce stepped up as the Rams' go-to receiver and caught 13 touchdown passes.

FACTS AND FIGURES

CONFERENCE/DIVISION	NFC West
FIRST YEAR IN NFL	1937
STADIUM/CAPACITY/SURFACE	Trans World Dome (66,000) /Artificial
FORMER CITIES/NICKNAMES	Cleveland Rams (1937-45); Los Angeles Rams (1946-94)
NFL CHAMPIONSHIPS	1945, 1951
SUPER BOWL CHAMPIONSHIPS	None

PLAYING RECORD	W	L	T	PCT
Regular Season	405	358	20	.530
Playoffs (22 Appearances)	13	20	0	.394

San Francisco 49ers

FIVE AND COUNTING

If you want to talk history with a 49ers fan, you might as well start in 1981, the preferred beginning of football time in San Francisco. The third season of the Bill Walsh-Joe Montana era; the first season of redemption after 31 years of NFL futility; the start of a run that eventually would produce five Super Bowl championships.

That magic season was just what the doctor ordered for victory-starved fans who had watched their 49ers suffer through four consecutive sub-.500 seasons and seven out of eight. Those fans had witnessed only three Western Division winners (1970, 1971 and 1972) in a franchise history that traced its roots to the old All-America Football Conference.

But 1981 would be different. With Montana, a third-round draft pick out of Notre Dame, operating Walsh's innovative controlled-passing offense, the 49ers pranced to a 13-3 regular-season record and defeated the New York Giants in the opening round of the playoffs.

It was in the NFC Championship Game against Dallas that Montana would set the tone for the 1980s and begin carving out his special place in history. With the 49ers trailing 27-21 with about five minutes remaining, Montana drove his team 89 yards and connected with a leaping Dwight Clark in the end zone for a dramatic winning touchdown. The 49ers concluded their first championship with a 26-21 victory over Cincinnati in Super Bowl XVI.

More would follow. Blessed with an ever-changing cast of talented offensive players (Clark, Freddie Solomon, Roger Craig, Jerry Rice, John Taylor, Randy Cross) and complemented by Pro Bowl-caliber defenders (Hacksaw Reynolds, Fred Dean, Michael Carter, Ronnie Lott, Eric Wright) the Montana-Walsh combination clicked for two more Super Bowl victories—after the 1984 and 1988 seasons—and Montana won another (after 1989) under the direction of George Seifert.

When Montana passed the quarterbacking baton to Steve Young in 1991, everybody expected a downturn in the 49ers' fortunes. Everybody was wrong. Young won four straight passing titles, guided the 49ers to NFC Championship Game appearances in 1992 and 1993 and sparked the franchise's fifth Super Bowl victory after the 1994 season. He fired a record six touchdown passes—including three to Rice and two to Ricky Watters—in a 49-26 victory over San Diego.

The 49ers were upset by Green Bay in the 1995 playoffs, after going 11-5 in the regular season, but their offensive guns remain loaded, they're defensively sound and they're experienced. The "Team of the 1980s" appears capable of battling Dallas for honors as the "Team of the 1990s."

 49ers gold: Steve Young was the cornerstone of the NFL's top team in 1994. San Francisco's quarterback was the MVP as the 49ers won Super Bowl XXIX.

FACTS AND FIGURES

CONFERENCE/DIVISION	NFC West
FIRST YEAR IN NFL	1950 (AAFC 1946-49)
STADIUM/CAPACITY/SURFACE	3Com Park (69,497) /Grass
FORMER CITIES/NICKNAMES	None
NFL CHAMPIONSHIPS	1981, 1984, 1988, 1989, 1994 (all Super Bowls)

PLAYING RECORD	W	L	T	PCT
Regular Season	356	281	13	.558
Playoffs (17 Appearances)	21	12	0	.636

Tampa Bay Buccaneers

ONWARD AND UPWARD

The low and high points in the Buccaneers' short history occurred within a three-year span. One minute they were the undisputed weaklings of the NFL, the next minute they were one of its tough guys.

When the Bucs were born in 1976 as the baby of Florida attorney Hugh Culverhouse, everybody expected them to suffer the expansion blues. So it wasn't surprising when they failed to win a game in their first season. But the streak would reach record proportions at 20, then 25, then 26. Tampa Bay finally broke through late in the 1977 season with a 33-14 victory at New Orleans and celebrated its success with a season-closing 17-7 home win over St. Louis.

A 5-11 record in 1978 did not prepare fans for what would happen next. The Buccaneers opened the 1979 season 5-0 and went on to win the NFC Central Division with a 10-6 record. But the Bucs didn't stop there. They posted a playoff victory over Philadelphia before losing to the Rams in the NFC Championship Game.

The surprising Bucs were a good balance of offense and defense. Quarterback Doug Williams passed for 2,448 yards, Ricky Bell ran for 1,263 more. The defense was built around end Lee Roy Selmon, the team's first-ever draft choice in 1976. Linebacker Richard Wood and backs Cedric Brown and Mike Washington gave Selmon plenty of support.

After a down season, the Bucs added linebacker Hugh Green and running back James Wilder. They bounced back to win another division title in 1981 and made consecutive postseason appearances, both of which ended with first-round losses to Dallas. And just like that it was over. No more division titles. Twelve consecutive seasons of double-digit losses. Thirteen without a postseason appearance. Five unsuccessful coaches.

Coach No. 6 arrived after Sam Wyche's final team struggled to a 7-9 record in 1995. Tony Dungy, a defensive specialist, finds himself in good position to return the Bucs to a playoff routine, thanks to such cornerstone youngsters as quarterback Trent Dilfer and running back Errict Rhett, who has topped 1,000 yards in each of his first two seasons. Dungy also has talented wide receiver Alvin Harper and a defense that showed signs of progress in 1995.

Whether those weapons will be enough to reverse 13 seasons of futility remain to be seen. But a winning attitude under a new coach sometimes can work wonders.

On the run: Young running back Errict Rhett, a two-time 1,000-yard rusher, could carry the improving Buccaneers back into the NFL playoffs.

FACTS AND FIGURES

CONFERENCE/DIVISION	NFC Central
FIRST YEAR IN NFL	1976
STADIUM/CAPACITY/SURFACE	Tampa Stadium (74,296)/Grass
FORMER CITIES/NICKNAMES	None
SUPER BOWL CHAMPIONSHIPS	None

PLAYING RECORD	W	L	T	PCT
Regular Season	94	213	1	.307
Playoffs (3 Appearances)	1	3	0	.250

Washington Redskins

A TOUGH ACT TO FOLLOW

When Joe Gibbs decided to quit in 1992 after 12 years as coach of the Redskins, he left with a legacy that may never be matched in Washington: 10 winning seasons, four NFC championships and three Super Bowl titles, more than any team except San Francisco over that span. So what did Richie Petitbon do for an encore? He coached the 1993 Redskins to a 4-12 disaster. Enter Norv Turner, who took over in 1994 and began a rebuilding program he hopes will produce a winning legacy of his own. Turner has a foundation in place, but progress has not come without pain.

With a rookie quarterback tandem of Heath Shuler and Gus Frerotte, aging go-to receiver Henry Ellard, a listless running game and a porous defense, the 1994 Redskins struggled to a 3-13 record. But the addition of free-agent running back Terry Allen and several key defenders led to a 6-10 1995 improvement and life could get a lot easier with a few more defensive additions.

Gibbs had a lot more to work with when he took the coaching reins in 1981 from Jack Pardee. He had a beefy offensive line called the "Hogs," a powerful running back in John Riggins, a heady quarterback in Joe Theismann and a receiving corps that included Art Monk and Alvin Garrett. The defense, anchored by end Dexter Manley and tackle Dave Butz, was deep and talented.

With that cast of characters and new receiver Charlie Brown, Washington dominated the NFC in 1982 and powered past Miami in Super Bowl XVII, winning the franchise's first NFL championship in 40 years. The Redskins almost repeated in 1983, advancing to the Super Bowl before losing to the Los Angeles Raiders.

As the cast changed, the winning continued. The 1987 Redskins earned their second Super Bowl victory, this time behind quarterback Doug Williams and receivers Monk, Gary Clark and Ricky Sanders. Three years later, quarterback Mark Rypien emerged as the game-breaker in a Super Bowl victory over Buffalo. That ended Gibbs' run of three championships in 11 seasons, one more than the Redskins had won in their previous 45-year Washington history.

Those first two NFL titles had been orchestrated by sensational quarterback Sammy Baugh in 1937 and 1942. But from 1943 to 1970, the Redskins managed only seven winning records.

George Allen arrived in 1971 and, with the help of such players as quarterback Sonny Jurgensen, running back Larry Brown, receiver Charley Taylor and safety Ken Houston, enjoyed seven consecutive winning seasons, reaching the playoffs five times and the Super Bowl once-a 14-7 loss to Miami after the 1972 campaign. Gibbs took over three years after Allen's 1977 finale.

FACTS AND FIGURES

CONFERENCE/DIVISION	NFC East
FIRST YEAR IN NFL	1932
STADIUM/CAPACITY/SURFACE	RFK Memorial Stadium (56,454)/Grass
FORMER CITIES/NICKNAMES	Boston Braves (1932); Boston Redskins (1933-36)
NFL CHAMPIONSHIPS	1937, 1942
SUPER BOWL CHAMPIONSHIPS	1982, 1987, 1991

PLAYING RECORD	W	L	T	PCT
Regular Season	439	385	26	.532
Playoffs (19 Appearances)	21	14	0	.600

 Coming attraction: Young quarterback Heath Shuler could be Washington's ticket to an exciting and prosperous future.

NFL Fans

Four-ring runner: As well as winning four Super Bowls rings, Franco Harris is the Pittsburgh Steelers' all-time rushing leader with 11,950 yards.

They're the one constant in the National Football League's universe, the electricity that illuminates its game. They energize and re-energize it with their special talents, draw attention to it with their brilliance.

Players come and players go, but the stars will shine forever. In our memories. In our hearts. In our record books.

Who can forget the stutter-stepping of Walter Payton? The powerful determination of Jim Brown? The graceful pass-catching artistry of Lynn Swann? The frightful intensity of Dick Butkus and Ray Nitschke? The winning legacies of Otto Graham and Bart Starr?

Texas hero: Defensive tackle Bob Lilly, was born, raised and educated in Texas, so he was a natural to be the Dallas Cowboys' first-ever draft pick.

Because those images stick in our minds and make us lust for more, professional football has grown into the No 1 spectator sport in the United States. One of football's greatest assets has been the impact its star players have on fan interest.

Sports has always needed its superstars and the NFL has provided a steady succession since the arrival of Red Grange, Ernie Nevers and Bronko Nagurski in the 1920s and 1930s. And, conversely, the brilliance of those stars often has been dictated by the needs of the game.

Reach for the Stars

When rules were made to encourage more passing in the 1930s, quarterbacks like Sammy Baugh and Sid Luckman began mesmerizing a growing fan base with unprecedented aerial displays. When the NFL needed help in its battle with the All-America Football Conference after World War II, runners like Charley Trippi and Steve Van Buren joined such quarterbacks as Bobby Layne and Bob Waterfield in a new talent explosion.

The Cleveland Browns ruled the 1950s with an all-star cast featuring Graham, Lou Groza, Marion Motley, Frank Gatski and Dante Lavelli, and the Green Bay Packers dominated the 1960s behind Starr and supporting stars Paul Hornung, Jerry Kramer, Jim Taylor, Forrest Gregg, Willie Davis and Herb Adderley.

All through football history, the game has been bolstered by unexpected individual feats—athletic performances previously beyond comprehension. When Chicago's Beattie Feathers became the NFL's first 1,000-yard rusher in 1934, everyone gasped. When Brown ran for 1,527 yards in 1958 and 1,863 five years later, everyone was astounded. And when Simpson topped 2,000 yards in 1973, everyone watched in disbelief.

Others claimed the spotlight with great individual performances. Colts quarterback Johnny Unitas threw at least one touchdown pass in 47 straight games from 1956 to 1960. The Bears' Luckman was the first quarterback to pass for seven touchdowns in a single game in 1943. Baltimore's Lenny Moore, one of Unitas' favorite targets, set a record by scoring touchdowns in 18 consecutive games from 1963-65. John Riggins of the Redskins scored 24 touchdowns in the 1983 season. And Walter Payton of the Bears ran for a single-game record 275 yards in 1977.

Miami featured the running back tandem of Larry Csonka, Jim Kiick and Mercury Morris, which led the Dolphins to a perfect 17-0 season in 1972 and consecutive Super Bowl victories. Even more fearsome was the Pittsburgh Steel Curtain that shrouded the NFL in the late 1970s, producing four Super Bowl titles in six years with a defense featuring Mean Joe Greene, LC Greenwood, Mel Blount, Dwight White and the Hall of Fame linebacking duo of Jack Ham and Jack Lambert.

For pure viewing pleasure, you couldn't go wrong with the grace and consistency of receivers like Don Hutson and Paul Warfield, the power and brute force of linemen like Ron Mix and Roosevelt Brown, the strength and intensity of defenders like Bob Lilly and Buck Buchanan, the speed and power of running backs like Riggins, Earl Campbell and Franco Harris and the combination running-passing skills of quarterbacks like Fran Tarkenton and Roger Staubach.

But nobody could fill a spotlight quite like New York Jets quarterback Joe Namath. Broadway Joe's powerful right arm helped the American Football League's Jets prosper in the years leading up to the merger with the NFL and his "I guarantee a victory" speech fueled one of the greatest upsets in sports history—the Jets' 16-7 victory over the Baltimore Colts in Super Bowl III.

The memories, and the stars, indeed will shine forever.

Piloting the Jets: Joe Namath was a New York sportswriter's dream: brash, controversial, glamorous and, most importantly, successful. He "guaranteed" the Jets' Super Bowl III victory.

Troy Aikman

★★★★★ **ENJOYING THE SUPER LIFE**

Special delivery: Troy Aikman has earned five successive Pro Bowl bids as the leader of the powerful Dallas Cowboys.

Troy Aikman has experienced life at both ends of the professional football spectrum. His status as quarterback of the three-time Super Bowl-champion Dallas Cowboys is tempered by memories of a humbling 1-15 rookie season—a memory that helps keep everything in perspective.

"I have one 1-15 season in me, and then I'm done," Aikman says. "That made me appreciate the NFL and understand how difficult it is to win."

To say that Aikman, who played collegiately at Oklahoma and UCLA, entered the NFL under difficult circumstances is a massive understatement. As the first overall pick of the 1989 draft, the strong-armed youngster was hailed as the "next Roger Staubach" by down-and-out Cowboys fans. And new Coach Jimmy Johnson fanned the speculation by pushing his $11.2-million quarterback into the heat of battle.

In the 11 games Aikman started as a rookie, the Cowboys were winless and much of his first season was spent on his back, looking up at the world through bleary eyes. The perspective that came from the experience was painful, but it also was invaluable during his transformation from a first-year caterpillar into an NFL butterfly.

When running back Emmitt Smith arrived in 1990 and Johnson began filling key positions around his quarterback (wide receivers Michael Irvin and Alvin Harper, tight end Jay Novacek, a huge offensive line), life improved quickly. The 1990 Cowboys jumped to 7-9 and the 1991 team, with a poised, mistake-free Aikman as its centerpiece, won 11 of 16 games before suffering a divisional playoff loss to Detroit.

There would be no postseason losses in 1992 or 1993 as Aikman directed the Cowboys to consecutive NFC Championship Game victories over San Francisco and Super Bowl victories over Buffalo. Super Bowl XXVII, a 52-17 rout of the Bills, belonged to Aikman, who completed 22 of 30 passes for 273 yards and four touchdowns en route to MVP honors.

> ## "He can throw the heck out of the football, and he never complains"
> ROGER STAUBACH

After a 1994 loss to the 49ers in the NFC Championship Game, the Cowboys, now coached by Barry Switzer, returned to the Super Bowl spotlight in 1995, defeating Pittsburgh, 27-17. Through it all, Aikman has accepted life as the unspectacular director of a machine-like offense that appears to operate on its own—not unlike the Roger Staubach and Bart Starr offenses of yesteryear.

"He can throw the heck out of the football, and he never complains," Staubach says. "He could put up numbers like Dan Marino because he has that much talent."

But the soft-spoken Aikman prefers the Super Bowls—and he leads his teammates with a team-first attitude that makes such success possible. His 62.8 percent completion percentage defines a career that has produced a 70-39 regular-season record in games he has started. That's not bad when you consider he started off 0-11.

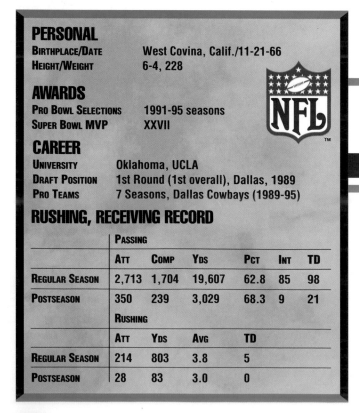

PERSONAL

BIRTHPLACE/DATE   West Covina, Calif./11-21-66
HEIGHT/WEIGHT   6-4, 228

AWARDS

PRO BOWL SELECTIONS   1991-95 seasons
SUPER BOWL MVP   XXVII

CAREER

UNIVERSITY   Oklahoma, UCLA
DRAFT POSITION   1st Round (1st overall), Dallas, 1989
PRO TEAMS   7 Seasons, Dallas Cowbays (1989-95)

RUSHING, RECEIVING RECORD

	PASSING					
	ATT	COMP	YDS	PCT	INT	TD
REGULAR SEASON	2,713	1,704	19,607	62.8	85	98
POSTSEASON	350	239	3,029	68.3	9	21
	RUSHING					
	ATT	YDS	AVG	TD		
REGULAR SEASON	214	803	3.8	5		
POSTSEASON	28	83	3.0	0		

Eric Dickerson

★★★★★★★ **MAN ON THE RUN**

In the clear: Eric Dickerson set the NFL single-season rushing record in 1984 when he ran for 2,105 yards for the Los Angeles Rams.

The first thing you noticed about running back Eric Dickerson was the glide. His feet seemed to hydroplane over a football field like a speedboat barely touching water. When Dickerson exploded through the line, nobody even felt an aftershock.

That glide was only one of Dickerson's gifts. Of more importance were his ability to accelerate through an opening and the unexplainable instinct that allowed him to rush for 13,259 career yards, second only to Walter Payton's all-time record of 16,726.

"I can't remember seeing any back with more talent than Eric," said Hall of Fame running back OJ Simpson midway through the 1984 season. "And that includes myself and Gale Sayers. He is the best I've seen, and I mean ever."

"Every time Eric gets the ball, I say, 'Oh my God, he has a chance to break it.'"

FORMER RAMS COACH JOHN ROBINSON

Ironically, Dickerson was on his way to the greatest single-season rushing total in NFL history (2,105 yards) when Simpson offered that assessment. Dickerson's 16-game total would break Simpson's 14-game 2,003-yard effort of 1973—the only other 2,000-yard performance in NFL history.

Dickerson, who was selected out of Southern Methodist University by the Los Angeles Rams with the second overall pick of the 1983 draft, had set the stage for that 1984 explosion with record-shattering rookie totals for rushing attempts (390), yards (1,808) and touchdowns (18).

PERSONAL	
BIRTHPLACE/DATE	Sealy, Tex/9-2-60
HEIGHT/WEIGHT	6-3, 220

AWARDS	
PRO BOWL SELECTIONS	1983-84, 1986-89 seasons
SUPER BOWL MVP	None

CAREER	
UNIVERSITY	Southern Methodist
DRAFT POSITION	1st Round (2nd overall), L.A. Rams, 1983
PRO TEAMS	11 Seasons, Los Angeles Rams (1983-87); Indianapolis Colts (1987-91); Los Angeles Raiders (1992); Atlanta Falcons (1993)

RUSHING, RECEIVING RECORD

	RUSHING				RECEIVING		
	ATT	YDS	AVG	TD	NO	YDS	TD
REGULAR SEASON	2,996	13,259	4.4	90	281	2,137	6
POSTSEASON	148	724	4.9	3	19	91	1

"Every time Eric gets the ball, I say, 'Oh my God, he has a chance to break it,'" marveled former Rams coach John Robinson. "Whenever he doesn't do something unbelievable, you're disappointed."

Dickerson didn't stop running after 1984. For seven consecutive seasons he passed the 1,000-yard barrier, another NFL record. His lowest total during that span was 1,234.

When relations broke down between Dickerson and the Rams over a contract in 1987, he became the focal point of a different kind of record. He was traded to Indianapolis as part of a three-team, 10-player deal that netted the Rams two players and six draft choices.

The change of scenery did not have an immediate effect on Dickerson's production. He finished off his fifth 1,000-yard season in 1987 and added two more for the Colts before injuries and age began taking their toll.

Dickerson, a six-time Pro Bowl invitee, concluded his career in 1993 after one-season stints in Los Angeles (with the Raiders) and Atlanta.

Tony Dorsett

★★★★★★★★★ **LITTLE BIG MAN**

PERSONAL
BIRTHPLACE/DATE   Rochester, Pa/4-7-54
HEIGHT/WEIGHT   5-11/185

AWARDS
PRO BOWL SELECTIONS   1978, 1981-83 seasons
SUPER BOWL MVP   None

CAREER
UNIVERSITY   Pittsburgh
DRAFT POSITION   1st Round (2nd overall), Dallas, 1977
PRO TEAMS   12 Seasons, Dallas Cowboys (1977-87);
                   Denver Broncos (1988)

RUSHING, RECEIVING RECORD

	RUSHING				RECEIVING		
	ATT	YDS	AVG	TD	NO	YDS	TD
REGULAR SEASON	2,936	12,739	4.3	77	398	3,554	13
POSTSEASON	302	1,383	4.6	9	46	403	1

A t first glance, Tony Dorsett appeared out of place among the big, hard bodies of the National Football League. Most 5-foot-11, 185-pound running backs have an NFL career expectancy of two or three crunching hits.

But Dorsett was not your normal, everyday back. Blessed with incredible balance and an ability to suddenly change direction, he darted, he slashed, he cut against the grain and he masterfully avoided tacklers for 12 seasons en route to 12,739 yards and a third-place ranking on the all-time rushing charts.

Such success was nothing new for Touchdown Tony, who earned his nickname and a Heisman Trophy during four incredible seasons at the University of Pittsburgh. Dorsett broke or tied 14 NCAA records while running for an unprecedented 6,082 career yards, scoring 58 touchdowns and leading the Panthers to an unbeaten record and the 1976 national championship.

When the Dallas Cowboys selected Dorsett with the second overall pick of the 1977 draft, some observers predicted a short career with minimal success. Dorsett had other ideas.

For eight of his first nine seasons, Dorsett topped the 1,000-yard barrier while catching 338 passes. The only season of the nine under 1,000 was 1982, when the schedule was cut to nine games because of a players' strike.

And the Cowboys enjoyed success with Dorsett as their feature back. They reached the NFC Championship Game five times and played in two Super Bowls, winning one (XII). Dorsett's 1,383 postseason rushing yards rank second only to Franco Harris' 1,556.

"No matter what he had to do, he wasn't exerting much effort," marveled Dan Reeves, former Cowboys offensive coordinator and now coach of the New York Giants. "He had the great acceleration that means so much in football. And he could make the full-speed cut."

Dorsett, who was elected to the Pro Football Hall of Fame in 1994, was known for his big-play ability. His 99-yard dash against Minnesota late in the 1982 season stands as the longest run from scrimmage in NFL history.

But Dorsett's most amazing quality might have been his durability. He never sustained a serious injury and he missed just three games in a nine-year stretch from 1977-85. He finished his career at Denver in 1988, playing all 16 games and rushing for 703 yards.

There he goes: Tony Dorsett rushed for 12,739 yards in his career, third-best total in NFL history. He also ran for 77 touchdowns.

"He had the great acceleration." FORMER DENVER AND CURRENT GIANTS COACH DAN REEVES

John Elway

★★★★ ### ARMED AND DANGEROUS

A ny description of John Elway starts with his arm—that magnificent arm. It's not his only physical tool, but it's certainly the most impressive. "When he's running to his left, he can throw the ball 60 yards on one foot," marveled former Raiders cornerback Mike Haynes. "With a lot of mustard on it."

That arm has been delivering passes to National Football League receivers for 13 often-spectacular seasons. Over that span, Elway has completed 3,346 passes and he joined six other quarterbacks in the exclusive 40,000-yard club (41,706) in 1995.

The arm was so impressive that Elway was being touted as an athletic wonder even before his collegiate days at Stanford. The

Stalking horse: John Elway has lost in three Super Bowls, but without his heroics, the Denver Broncos would never have been close to the big game.

PERSONAL

BIRTHPLACE/DATE	Port Angeles, Wash/6-28-60
HEIGHT/WEIGHT	6-3/215

AWARDS

PRO BOWL SELECTIONS	1986-87, 1989, 1991, 1993-94 seasons
SUPER BOWL MVP	None

CAREER

UNIVERSITY	Stanford
DRAFT POSITION	1st Round (1st overall), Baltimore, 1983
PRO TEAMS	13 Seasons, Denver Broncos (1983-95)

PASSING, RUSHING RECORD

	PASSING					
	ATT	COMP	YDS	PCT	INT	TD
REGULAR SEASON	5,926	3,346	41,706	.565	191	225
POSTSEASON	384	200	3,019	.521	17	16
	RUSHING					
	ATT	YDS	AVG	TD		
REGULAR SEASON	637	2,846	4.3	27		
POSTSEASON	66	349	5.3	4		

Yankees were so impressed with his baseball ability that they picked him first in the 1981 June draft. Over his four seasons for the Cardinal, he delighted football scouts by passing for 9,349 yards and 77 touchdowns.

Baltimore made Elway the first overall choice of the 1983 NFL draft, ahead of such notables as Tony Eason, Jim Kelly, Todd Blackledge, Ken O'Brien and Dan Marino in the "Year of the Quarterback." But he refused to sign with the Colts, forcing a trade that transformed the Denver Broncos from also-rans to contenders.

By 1985, Elway was displaying the leadership abilities that would take the Broncos to five AFC Western Division titles and three AFC championships, a success record marred only by losses in all three Super Bowls. And over the course of Elway's career, he earned a reputation as one of the great comeback quarterbacks of all time.

"There's no question John is the greatest two-minute quarterback ever."

"There's no question John is the greatest two-minute quarterback ever," former Broncos coach Dan Reeves once said. "He's got that arm, and the point of a two-minute attack is that everybody in the world knows you're going to throw—and your arm is strong enough to do it anyway."

But "the arm" is not Elway's only weapon. He also is one of the game's most feared scramblers, a reputation Elway attributes to quick feet. His mad dashes have produced 2,846 career rushing yards, the fifth-best all-time figure among quarterbacks. They also have allowed him to avoid rushers and protect his body from hits that other quarterbacks are forced to endure.

"He's got the mobility of Fran Tarkenton and the arm of Joe Namath," said former Arizona Cardinals Coach Buddy Ryan.

A lethal combination.

John Hannah

★★★★★   ## A BLOCKING MACHINE

PERSONAL
BIRTHPLACE/DATE   Canton, Ga/4-4-51
HEIGHT/WEIGHT   6-3, 260

AWARDS
PRO BOWL SELECTIONS   1976, 1978-85 seasons
SUPER BOWL MVP   None

CAREER
UNIVERSITY   Alabama
DRAFT POSITION   1st Round (4th overall), New England, 1973
PRO TEAMS   13 Seasons, New England Patriots (1973-85)

"He's one of the best linemen I've ever played against."

HALL OF FAME DEFENSIVE TACKLE RANDY WHITE

Contrary to rumors, Herb Hannah did not have a lucrative contract to produce football talent for Paul (Bear) Bryant's Alabama football machine. But it must have seemed that way to Southeastern Conference fans.

Sons John, Charley and David all took turns playing for the Crimson Tide, John earning a consensus All-America citation as an offensive guard and Charley and David earning all-conference honors as defensive tackles. The boys simply were following in the footsteps of their father, who played offensive tackle for Alabama and the New York Giants in the early 1950s.

John and Charley (a combined 520 pounds of muscle) went on to professional careers of their own, but that's where the comparisons end. Charley played 11 solid seasons with Tampa Bay and the Los Angeles Raiders. But John played at a different level over an outstanding 13-year career as a guard with the New England Patriots.

"He's one of the best linemen I've ever played against," said Hall of Fame defensive tackle Randy White, who made his living embarrassing offensive guards. "When you played against John, it was a major challenge. You had to keep your helmet strapped on tight."

There are plenty of defenders who didn't and had it knocked off by the intense Hannah. At 6-feet-3, 260 pounds, he was the outstanding run-blocker of his era. Not surprisingly, the Patriots thrived with a power running attack.

When Hannah, who was elected to the Pro Football Hall of Fame in 1991, stepped on the field, nobody doubted who was in control. "He always wanted to dominate and he did," recalled former Patriots quarterback Matt Cavanaugh. Hannah intimidated opponents quietly, with a businesslike, no-nonsense demeanor that never varied from play to play.

When a defender got out of line or a little too boisterous, Hannah delivered a quick message with his powerful forearm. He was most devastating in pulling situations, when he bulldozed unfortunate defensive ends or linebackers at full speed.

With Hannah leading the charge, the Patriots rushed for an NFL single-season record 3,165 yards in 1978. The 1985 Patriots powered their way to the AFC championship before losing to the Chicago Bears in Super Bowl XX.

When a recurring knee injury forced Hannah's retirement after the Super Bowl, he left with nine Pro Bowl citations and the respect of his coaches and peers. "You had better believe he was the best offensive lineman in the history of the NFL," said Jim Ringo, a Hall of Fame center and Hannah's former line coach.

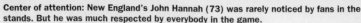

Center of attention: New England's John Hannah (73) was rarely noticed by fans in the stands. But he was much respected by everybody in the game.

★★★★★★★★★★★★★★★★

Steve Largent

★★★ ## THE CEREBRAL PASS-CATCHER

When Steve Largent's name came up in scouting reports, it usually was accompanied by such words as "heady," "cerebral" and "consistent." But at least one NFL defensive back took his description a step further.

"I call him the Albert Einstein of pass receivers," former Raiders cornerback Lester Hayes once said, "because he's always coming up with some kind of new space age route I've never seen before."

Largent, who caught 819 passes for 13,089 yards and 100 touchdowns over a sterling 14-year career for the Seattle Seahawks, was the thinking man's receiver. What he lacked in speed and athletic grace, he made up for with guile and savvy. Covering the wily Largent was a game of cat and mouse.

"Every time I play him, he pulls a new trick out of his bag," said cornerback Albert Lewis, then with the Chiefs.

"He's always thinking ahead, even though it might not seem that way to you when you cover him," said safety Ronnie Lott. "He might run a certain pattern and you cover him, and you might think that you're doing your job. But basically he's setting you up for the next play."

The essence of Largent's guile might have been that he was more physically gifted than everybody believed. He did not have great straightaway speed, but he had a lateral quickness that allowed him to make defenders look silly. He also had great balance, body control, hand/eye coordination and hands that seldom dropped a pass.

"Every time I play him, he pulls a new trick out of his bag."

CORNERBACK ALBERT LEWIS

Such qualities were lost on the Houston Oilers, who drafted Largent out of Tulsa with a fourth-round pick in 1976, took one look at him in training camp and shuffled him off to the expansion Seahawks. By 1978, Largent was making the Oilers and the rest of the NFL take note.

For eight of the next nine seasons (1978-1986), Largent topped the 1,000-yard barrier while embarking on an NFL-record consecutive games reception streak that would reach 177 (since broken). His only sub-1,000-yard efforts from 1978-87 were in strike-shortened seasons.

By the time Largent retired after the 1989 campaign, he owned NFL career records for most receptions, yards and touchdown catches—marks that since have been broken. He was elected to the Pro Football Hall of Fame in 1995. The only negative in a career that included seven Pro Bowl invitations was lack of team success. The best the Seahawks managed was an AFC Championship Game loss after the 1983 season.

Success is catching: Seattle wide receiver Steve Largent set NFL receiving records for number of catches, yards, touchdowns and consecutive games with passes caught, all now surpassed.

PERSONAL
BIRTHPLACE/DATE	Tulsa, Okla/9-28-54
HEIGHT/WEIGHT	5-11/191

AWARDS
PRO BOWL SELECTIONS	1978-79, 1981, 1984-87 seasons
SUPER BOWL MVP	None

CAREER
UNIVERSITY	Tulsa
DRAFT POSITION	4th Round (117th overall), Houston, 1976
PRO TEAMS	14 Seasons, Seattle Seahawks (1976-89)

RECEIVING RECORD
	No	YDS	AVG	LG	TD
REGULAR SEASON	819	13,089	16.0	74	100
POSTSEASON	23	433	18.8	56	4

Ronnie Lott

★★★★★

A DEFENSIVE LEGEND

PERSONAL
BIRTHPLACE/DATE   Albuquerque, NM/5-8-59
HEIGHT/WEIGHT   6-1/200

AWARDS
PRO BOWL SELECTIONS   1981-84, 1986-91 seasons
SUPER BOWL MVP   None

CAREER
UNIVERSITY   Southern California
DRAFT POSITION   1st Round (8th overall), San Francisco, 1981
PRO TEAMS   14 Seasons, San Francisco 49ers (1981-90); Los Angeles Raiders (1991-92); New York Jets (1993-94)
INTERCEPTIONS   Regular Season, 63. Postseason, 9.

The footsteps wide receivers often hear in their worst nightmares belong to Ronnie Lott. Lott, who completed his 14th and final NFL season in 1994 at age 35, is an NFL legend. He's also one of the greatest defensive backs ever to play the game.

"The guy's going to Canton (the Hall of Fame) on rollerskates," said New England Coach Bill Parcells. "I've seen my share of him first-hand. He's one of the best guys that's ever played. You're talking about one of my very favorite players ever."

That's a typical reaction to Lott. Love him, hate him. Love him because he's one of the most competitive, hard-hitting, resourceful players ever to put on a uniform. Hate him for the exact same reasons. He plays the game like the players from yesteryear. Receivers beware.

"When you see Ronnie taking out guys on film, it puts thoughts in the back of your mind," said former Cowboys tight end Doug Cosbie. "You know he's going to hit you and it's not going to be a

> "You know he's going to hit you and it's not going to be a whole lot of fun. It's like a prizefighter who has to face Mike Tyson."
>
> FORMER COWBOYS TIGHT END DOUG COSBIE

whole lot of fun. It's like a prizefighter who has to face Mike Tyson."

Lott, who is as soft-spoken off the field as he is crazy on it, plays with passion, throwing his 6-foot-1, 200-pound body at anybody who moves. He intimidates receivers, who often are more interested in protecting their ribs than catching the pass. He intimidates quarterbacks, who have seen him make 63 career interceptions, fifth on the all-time list. Whether covering a speedy receiver, blitzing a quarterback or chasing down an elusive ball carrier, Lott is a master of his art.

Lott, a cornerback and free safety over his outstanding career, was selected out of USC with the eighth overall pick of the 1981 draft. He quickly fit into San Francisco's blueprint for success and led the bruising 49ers defense that helped carve out four Super Bowl championships in the 1980s. Lott, who owns virtually every 49ers pass defense record, did not win any championships in shorter stints with the Los Angeles Raiders and the Jets, but he did earn another Pro Bowl citation with the Raiders in 1991, the 10th time he was honored in his first 11 seasons.

 Passing Lottery: Few teams dared to go deep on the San Francisco 49ers when Ronnie Lott was in the defensive backfield. He won four Super Bowl rings.

Dan Marino

★★★★★★

A PASSING FANCY

I t had been billed as the "Year of the Quarterback" and, sure enough, five well-armed college passers were snapped up within the first 24 picks of the NFL draft. John Elway, Todd Blackledge, Tony Eason, Jim Kelly, Ken O'Brien.

In retrospect, it's inconceivable that Dan Marino could be rated sixth on anybody's list of quarterbacks. Over the 13 seasons since he was selected 27th in the 1983 draft, Marino has conducted a record-setting aerial circus while establishing himself as the greatest passer in pro football history.

Former Miami Dolphins Coach Don Shula sometimes had to pinch himself when he thought about his good fortune. Marino, a pro-style quarterback at the University of Pittsburgh, had struggled through a difficult senior year (23 interceptions) while trying to learn a new offense. Five NFL teams backed off.

By the end of the 1983 season, it was clear they had made a big mistake. The rookie warmed up with 173 completions for 2,210 yards and 20 touchdowns. In 1984, he exploded into prominence, setting NFL single-season records for passing yards (5,084) and TD passes (48). The Dolphins rolled to a 14-2 regular-season record and defeated Pittsburgh in the AFC Championship Game before losing to San Francisco in Super Bowl XIX.

As the NFL watched the young quarterback in amazement, the intense Marino continued to terrorize NFL secondaries with 400-yard passing games and a flurry of TD bombs. He did it with a calm precision and unerring accuracy that shocked Shula.

"How can he play any better," Shula asked after Marino's monster 1984 season. "I don't know. I really don't know."

The poise and confidence Marino displayed in his first two seasons were remarkable. But so was his ability to read defenses and the physical tools he used to pick them apart.

Foremost is the release. "The quickest arm I've ever seen," marveled Shula. With a flick of the wrist, Marino can avoid the rush and deliver a 30-yard pass like a bullet to an open receiver. The release also allows the 6-foot-4 Marino to see the entire field, not just his primary receivers. And the patience keeps his interceptions down, compensating for his one flaw—below-average speed.

As the years pile up, so do the career numbers. By the end of the 1995 season, Marino ranked first all-time in completions (3,913), attempts (6,531), passing yards (48,841), touchdown passes (352) and 300-yard passing games (52). And he's showing no signs of slowing down. Before he's through, Marino should own his own section of the NFL record book.

"The quickest arm I've ever seen."

PERSONAL
BIRTHPLACE/DATE	Pittsburgh, Pa./9-15-61
HEIGHT/WEIGHT	6-4/224

AWARDS
PRO BOWL SELECTIONS	1983-87, 1991-92, 1994 seasons
SUPER BOWL MVP	None

CAREER
UNIVERSITY	Pittsburgh
DRAFT POSITION	1st Round (27th overall), Miami, 1983
PRO TEAMS	13 Seasons, Miami Dolphins (1983-95)

PASSING RECORD
	ATT	COMP	YDS	PCT	INT	TD
REGULAR SEASON	6,531	3,913	48,841	.599	200	352
POSTSEASON	518	291	3,600	.562	17	29

 Press release: Dan Marino's passing style is so quick-fire he rarely gets sacked. His quick release demands the Miami Dolphins have fast wide receivers.

Art Monk

THE QUIET SUPERSTAR

PERSONAL
BIRTHPLACE/DATE   White Plains, NY/ 12-5-57
HEIGHT/WEIGHT   6-3/210

AWARDS
PRO BOWL SELECTIONS   1984-86 seasons
SUPER BOWL MVP   None

CAREER
UNIVERSITY   Syracuse
DRAFT POSITION   1st Round (18th overall), Washington, 1980
PRO TEAMS   16 Seasons, Washington Redskins (1980-93);
                  New York Jets (1994) Philadelphia Eagles (1995)

RECEIVING RECORD

	No.	YDS	AVG	LG	TD
REGULAR SEASON	940	12,721	13.5	79t	68
POSTSEASON	70	1,062	15.2	48	7

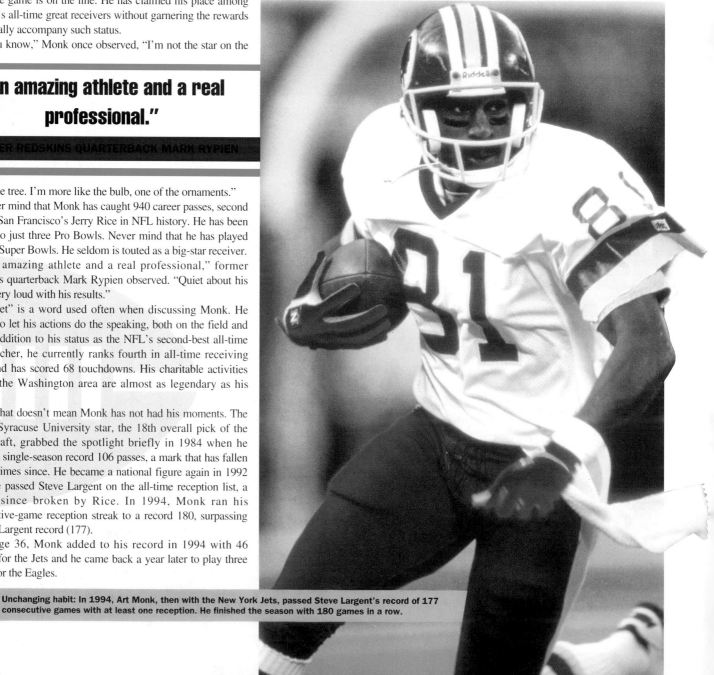

t's not that Art Monk doesn't get the respect he deserves. It's just that he gets it quietly, without the spotlight that shines on his big-play contemporaries. But National Football League defensive backs know all about Monk. So do appreciative Washington fans who watched him perform workmanlike pass-catching duties for 14 seasons before losing him as a 1994 free agent to the New York Jets.

While wide receivers like Jerry Rice, James Lofton and Sterling Sharpe have piled up big numbers and generated the headlines, Monk has been content to labor in their shadows.

He has built a career by catching passes in the middle of the field, a no-man's land of broken ribs and shattered careers. He has earned a reputation as a go-to receiver, the man who will make the difficult catch when the game is on the line. He has claimed his place among football's all-time great receivers without garnering the rewards that usually accompany such status.

"You know," Monk once observed, "I'm not the star on the

"An amazing athlete and a real professional."

FORMER REDSKINS QUARTERBACK MARK RYPIEN

top of the tree. I'm more like the bulb, one of the ornaments."

Never mind that Monk has caught 940 career passes, second only to San Francisco's Jerry Rice in NFL history. He has been invited to just three Pro Bowls. Never mind that he has played in three Super Bowls. He seldom is touted as a big-star receiver.

"An amazing athlete and a real professional," former Redskins quarterback Mark Rypien observed. "Quiet about his work, very loud with his results."

"Quiet" is a word used often when discussing Monk. He prefers to let his actions do the speaking, both on the field and off. In addition to his status as the NFL's second-best all-time pass-catcher, he currently ranks fourth in all-time receiving yards and has scored 68 touchdowns. His charitable activities around the Washington area are almost as legendary as his career.

But that doesn't mean Monk has not had his moments. The former Syracuse University star, the 18th overall pick of the 1980 draft, grabbed the spotlight briefly in 1984 when he caught a single-season record 106 passes, a mark that has fallen several times since. He became a national figure again in 1992 when he passed Steve Largent on the all-time reception list, a record since broken by Rice. In 1994, Monk ran his consecutive-game reception streak to a record 180, surpassing another Largent record (177).

At age 36, Monk added to his record in 1994 with 46 catches for the Jets and he came back a year later to play three games for the Eagles.

Unchanging habit: In 1994, Art Monk, then with the New York Jets, passed Steve Largent's record of 177 consecutive games with at least one reception. He finished the season with 180 games in a row.

Joe Montana

NO ORDINARY JOE

When the San Francisco 49ers spent a third-round 1979 draft pick (the 82nd overall) on a young Notre Dame quarterback named Joe Montana, they could not have known the impact of their decision. A struggling franchise was investing in a future legend.

A decade later, the 49ers would be proud owners of a record-tying four Super Bowl titles and "Montana Magic" would be synonymous with late-game heroics and championship-level performance.

"He's the greatest big-game player I've seen, period."

FORMER 49ERS CENTER RANDY CROSS

It's hard to dispute the facts. In his 16-year career with the 49ers and Kansas City Chiefs, Montana completed 3,409 passes for 40,551 yards. He was a three-time Super Bowl Most Valuable Player and is holder of virtually every Super Bowl passing record. He is the only quarterback to pass for more than 5,000 postseason yards. He is an eight-time Pro Bowl invitee and he engineered 31 winning fourth-quarter comebacks, including playoffs.

PERSONAL
BIRTHPLACE/DATE	New Eagle. Pa / 6-11-56
HEIGHT/WEIGHT	6-2/205

AWARDS
PRO BOWL SELECTIONS	1981, 1983-85, 1987, 1989-90, 1993 seasons
SUPER BOWL MVP	XVI, XIX, XXIV

CAREER
UNIVERSITY	Notre Dame
DRAFT POSITION	3rd Round (82nd overall), San Francisco, 1979
PRO TEAMS	16 Seasons, San Francisco 49ers (1979-92); Kansas City Chiefs (1993-94)

PASSING, RUSHING RECORD

PASSING						
	ATT	COMP	YDS	PCT	INT	TD
REGULAR SEASON	5,391	3,409	40,551	.632	139	273
POSTSEASON	734	460	5,772	.627	21	45

RUSHING				
	ATT	YDS	AVG	TD
REGULAR SEASON	457	1,674	3.7	20
POSTSEASON	63	310	4.9	2

Not bad for a quarterback with only slightly above-average arm strength and speed. The Montana legend was built around quick feet, a quicker mind and the determination and ability to succeed when everything is on the line.

"He is clearly the best quarterback in football today and maybe the best in many years," marveled former 49ers coach Bill Walsh after watching Montana direct a Super Bowl XIX victory over Miami a decade ago.

"I just hope now they'll stop saying, 'He's right up there with the best,'" former 49ers center Randy Cross said after Montana's 10-yard touchdown pass to John Taylor with 34 seconds remaining had given the 49ers a 20-16 victory over Cincinnati in Super Bowl XXIII. "He's the greatest big-game player I've seen, period."

After a serious elbow injury sidelined Montana for the entire 1991 season and all but one game in 1992, he resurrected his career in Kansas City, where he was greeted like a conquering hero. Trying to guide the Chiefs to their first Super Bowl since 1970, Montana got them as far as the 1993 AFC Championship Game before they stumbled at Buffalo. He also guided Kansas City to the playoffs in 1994.

Finally, in the spring of 1995, the 38-year-old Montana, still wishing he had played in one more Super Bowl announced his retirement. The NFL will miss him.

Redefining the position: For many people, Joe Montana is the greatest quarterback in NFL history. His three Super Bowl MVP awards are a record.

Anthony Muñoz

★★★

POWER IN THE TRENCHES

PERSONAL
BIRTHPLACE/DATE   Ontario, Calif/8-19-58
HEIGHT/WEIGHT   6-6/285

AWARDS
PRO BOWL SELECTIONS   1981-91 seasons
SUPER BOWL MVP   None

CAREER
UNIVERSITY   Southern California
DRAFT POSITION   1st Round (3rd overall), Cincinnati, 1980
PRO TEAMS   13 Seasons, Cincinnati Bengals (1980-92)

Who's the greatest offensive tackle of all time? Hall of Fame tackle Mike McCormack has a good idea. "Anthony Muñoz was the epitome of what an NFL offensive lineman should be," he said. "I've never seen one better."

McCormack's view is supported by defensive end Greg Townsend, a two-time Pro Bowl performer for the Los Angeles Raiders. "He's the best tackle I've ever seen," Townsend said.

From his days as an All-American at USC through his 13-year career with the Cincinnati Bengals, Muñoz earned such accolades from impressed viewers. The late Paul Brown, one of the greatest judges of football talent in NFL history, recalled watching Muñoz play for the Trojans in the 1980 Rose Bowl against Ohio State. "The guy was so big and so good it was a joke," he said.

With Brown providing that reference, the Bengals selected Muñoz with the third overall pick of the 1980 draft and he quickly began throwing his 285 pounds around with enthusiastic abandon.

Muñoz, showing amazing agility and foot quickness for his 6-foot-6 frame, dominated defenders with his "attack" philosophy. "He has a defensive mentality on offense," Townsend once said. "He has this killer instinct to get his man and put him away."

Whether opening holes for Cincinnati runners or dropping back to protect the quarterback, Muñoz usually won the war of the trenches. He was like an impenetrable wall. His quickness, toughness and consistency impressed teammates and opponents alike, earning him 11 invitations to the Pro Bowl. From 1980-91, he was snubbed only once—his rookie season.

> ## "He has this killer instinct to get his man and put him away."
> **DEFENSIVE END GREG TOWNSEND**

With Muñoz providing an offensive anchor, the Bengals rose to prominence, losing to San Francisco in Super Bowl XVI (26-21) and Super Bowl XXIII (20-16)—the only close calls for the 49ers in their five Super Bowl victories.

But of all of his awards, Muñoz said he was most proud of the 1991 NFL Man of the Year citation that annually honors role models, both on and off the field. Muñoz has been active in many charitable activities, including drug and alcohol programs in the Cincinnati area.

When he retired after the 1992 season, a collective sigh of relief could be heard from NFL defensive coordinators who never saw the charitable side of this football giant.

No pussycat: Offensive tackle Anthony Muñoz was a first-round draft pick in 1980 by the Cincinnati Bengals. He was voted to 11 Pro Bowls.

Walter Payton

MR. VERSATILITY

He was known affectionately as "Sweetness." But the Walter Payton who graced National Football League fields for 13 record-setting seasons was anything but. Payton, the Chicago Bears' primary offensive weapon from 1975-87 and the most prolific running back in the history of the game, was a collision waiting to happen, a defense's worst nightmare. Not only would Payton slash his 5-foot-10, 200-pound body through the tiniest of cracks in a defensive line and outsprint speedy linebackers to the corner, he would dish out punishing hits to destructive-minded tacklers.

San Diego Chargers General Manager Bobby Beathard called Payton the most complete player who ever played in the NFL. Mike Ditka, Payton's coach for six seasons, seconded that notion.

"He's the most gifted athlete I've ever seen," Ditka said. For all of his individual success, which included a record 275-yard rushing effort against Minnesota in 1977, Payton labored for a mediocre team much of his career. The Bears earned wild-card playoff spots in 1977 and 1979, but otherwise were also-rans until awakening in the mid-1980s.

Payton did go out in a blaze of glory. The Bears won NFC Central Division championships from 1984-87 and Payton was able to showcase his talents in Super Bowl XX, a 46-10 Bears victory over New England.

Payton retired as the holder of 23 team records and 8 NFL marks, including 110 rushing touchdowns. The 10-time 1,000-yard rusher also played in nine Pro Bowls. He was elected to the Pro Football Hall of Fame in 1993.

> ## "He's the most gifted athlete I've ever seen."
> FORMER BEARS COACH MIKE DITKA

But Payton's legacy goes beyond the record 16,726 rushing yards (3,467 ahead of second-place Eric Dickerson) he compiled after coming out of Jackson State as the fourth overall draft pick in 1975. The black-shirted No. 34 also was one of professional football's most versatile talents—and one of its most willing to sacrifice for his team.

"As far as blocking, tackling, running, durability, intelligence, throwing, he does it all," said Bill Tobin, the Colts director of operations and a former Bears executive, a few years ago.

Tobin wasn't exaggerating. During the prime of Payton's career, scouts considered him the best blocking back in the league. Payton played in 174 consecutive regular-season games from his rookie 1975 season through 1986. He caught 492 NFL passes for 4,538 yards and set the NFL record for combined yardage (rushing, receiving and kick returns) with 21,803. And he even threw eight career touchdown passes and served as the Bears' backup punter and placekicker.

PERSONAL

BIRTHPLACE/DATE	Columbia, Miss / 7-25-54
HEIGHT/WEIGHT	5-10/200

AWARDS

PRO BOWL SELECTIONS	1976-80, 1983-86 seasons
SUPER BOWL MVP	None

CAREER

UNIVERSITY	Jackson State
DRAFT POSITION	1st Round (4th overall), Chicago, 1975
PRO TEAMS	13 Seasons, Chicago Bears (1975-87)

RUSHING, RECEIVING RECORD

	RUSHING				RECEIVING		
	ATT	YDS	AVG	TD	NO	YDS	TD
REGULAR SEASON	3,838	16,726	4.4	110	492	4,538	15
POSTSEASON	180	632	3.5	2	22	178	0

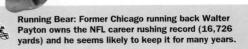

Running Bear: Former Chicago running back Walter Payton owns the NFL career rushing record (16,726 yards) and he seems likely to keep it for many years.

Jerry Rice

THE NATURAL

Perfect reception: San Francisco 49ers wide receiver Jerry Rice is generally acknowledged as the greatest wide receiver in the history of the NFL.

He wasn't anything special. He dropped passes, ran bad routes and sometimes looked out of control. Jerry Rice, the San Francisco 49ers' 1985 first-round draft pick out of tiny Mississippi Valley State University, looked like your average, everyday rookie wide receiver.

Until, that is, a late-season Monday night game when Rice exploded into national prominence with a 10-catch, 241-yard performance against the Los Angeles Rams. Over the next 10 seasons, Rice would help carry the 49ers to three Super Bowl championships while cementing his claim as the greatest wide receiver in the history of the game.

"I really want to be the all-time best receiver ever to play in the NFL."

JERRY RICE

The more-confident Rice that 49ers Coach Bill Walsh unleashed on the National Football League in 1986 was a devastating offensive weapon. He was a perfect combination of size, speed, grace and agility. Using his 6-foot-2 frame and long arms against smaller defensive backs, he pulled in the difficult passes. Fearless over the middle and sure-handed in a crowd, Rice had an extra gear that could separate him from the swiftest defender.

"He had the Paul Warfield grace, the Charley Taylor determination, the hands of (Fred) Biletnikoff," recalled teammate Ronnie Lott, an understanding defensive back. "He had the Dwight Clark work attitude. I just knew right away some good things were going to happen. I just didn't expect so many good things."

Rice had the same vision. "I really want to be the all-time best receiver ever to play in the NFL," he said early in his career.

It didn't take long to figure out that could really happen. Working in the 49ers' sophisticated offense and receiving passes from such quarterbacks as Joe Montana and Steve Young, Rice began piling up big numbers. When the 49ers completed their 1995 season, Rice owned virtually every receiving record.

He became the most prolific touchdown maker in NFL history, passing Walter Payton and Jim Brown, during San Francisco's 1994 Super Bowl run. In 1995 he passed Art Monk as the all-time leader in receptions (942). He also ranks first all-time in touchdown receptions (146) and receiving yards (15,123) and he set the single-season yardage record in 1995 with 1,848. Rice owns every major postseason, Super Bowl and Pro Bowl mark.

And he's only 33. By the time Rice is finished, he could warrant a special section in the NFL's record book. "He is not a normal human being," former teammate Randy Cross once said. He was right about that.

PERSONAL

BIRTHPLACE/DATE	Starkville, Miss./10-13-62
HEIGHT/WEIGHT	6-2/200

AWARDS

PRO BOWL SELECTIONS	1986-95 seasons
SUPER BOWL MVP	XXIII

CAREER

UNIVERSITY	Mississippi Valley State
DRAFT POSITION	1st Round (16th overall), San Francisco 49ers, 1985
PRO TEAMS	11 Seasons, San Francisco 49ers (1985-95)

RUSHING, RECEIVING RECORD

	RUSHING			
	ATT	YDS	AVG	TD
REGULAR SEASON	69	547	7.9	9
POSTSEASON	7	44	6.3	0

	RECEIVING				
	NO	YDS	AVG	LG	TD
REGULAR SEASON	942	15,123	16.1	96t	146
POSTSEASON	111	1,656	14.9	72t	17

Barry Sanders

★★★★★★★★★★

THE LION KING

I f Detroit's Barry Sanders is not the best running back in the National Football League, he's certainly the most exciting. Many coaches and players believe he's both. "He makes you stand on your toes any time he gets the ball," Lions Coach Wayne Fontes says. "You watch because you feel something big's about to happen."

Watching Sanders carry the ball is an adventure. Every run is filled with stops, starts, head fakes, jukes, quick cuts and broken tackles. Whether it nets one yard or 90, it electrifies the crowd—home or road. Sanders' quickness is startling, his balance and power inconceivable.

"Barry can flat-out embarrass anyone," says linebacker and former teammate Chris Spielman. And Sanders has embarrassed plenty of his opponents en route to two rushing titles and 1,000-yard performances in each of his seven NFL seasons.

The incredible quickness is complemented by a set of powerful legs that allow Sanders to break tackles and regain his balance when it appears he is going down. When he does get free, he has breakaway speed.

PERSONAL
BIRTHPLACE/DATE   Wichita, Kan./7-16-68
HEIGHT/WEIGHT   5-8/200

AWARDS
PRO BOWL SELECTIONS   1989-95 seasons
SUPER BOWL MVP   None

CAREER
UNIVERSITY   Oklahoma State (left after 3 seasons)
DRAFT POSITION   1st Round (3rd overall), Detroit, 1989
PRO TEAMS   7 Seasons, Detroit Lions (1989-95)

RUSHING, RECEIVING RECORD

	RUSHING				RECEIVING		
	ATT	YDS	AVG	TD	NO	YDS	TD
REGULAR SEASON	2,077	10,172	4.9	73	258	2,180	7
POSTSEASON	73	321	4.4	1	16	68	0

Nobody could have guessed that a squatty 5-foot-8, 200-pound body with tree-trunk legs would carry Sanders so far. But by his junior year at Oklahoma State University, he was confounding college defenses en route to the 1988 Heisman Trophy and 13 NCAA rushing and scoring records. When Sanders announced he would bypass his senior season, the Lions were waiting with the third overall pick of the draft.

"He makes you stand on your toes any time he gets the ball."

LIONS COACH WAYNE FONTES

The quiet, soft-spoken Sanders has been a worthy investment. He was unsure of his role in Detroit's run-and-shoot offense when he joined the team in 1989, but a 1,470-yard, 14-touchdown rookie season eliminated the doubts and 24 receptions for 282 yards enhanced his reputation as a versatile performer. That pattern would continue.

And Sanders, who already holds virtually every Lions career rushing record, would lead the playoff-starved team to a pair of NFC Central Division titles and four postseason appearances, giving him god-like status in Detroit. But his admirers are not confined to the Motor City.

"He's very special," said former Chicago coach Mike Ditka. "He reminds me of another player we used to have named Walter Payton."

That's pretty select company.

Hard to stop: One of the most amazing things about Barry Sanders' rushing style is the number of tacklers he avoids, both in a crowd and the open field.

★★★★★★★★★★★★★★★

Mike Singletary

★★★★★★★

ANOTHER BUTKUS

PERSONAL
BIRTHPLACE/DATE   Houston, Tex / 10-9-58
HEIGHT/WEIGHT   6-0/230

AWARDS
PRO BOWL SELECTIONS   1983-92 seasons
SUPER BOWL MVP   None

CAREER
UNIVERSITY   Baylor
DRAFT POSITION   2nd Round (38th overall), Chicago, 1981
PRO TEAMS   12 Seasons, Chicago Bears (1981-92)
SACKS   Regular Season, 19. Postseason, 1.

Mike Singletary, a Baylor University middle linebacker with professional aspirations, knew something that the National Football League scouts didn't know. "He was dead serious, very businesslike," said former Bears scout Jim Parmer, referring to a pre-draft interview. "He looked right at me and said, 'Mr Parmer, if you draft me, I'm going to be the best linebacker in the National Football League.' "

Despite Singletary's suspect size (6-foot, 230 pounds) and below-average speed, Parmer was impressed enough to recommend that the Bears take a chance. They grabbed him on the second round of the 1981 draft and nobody ever regretted the decision.

What the youngster lacked in size and speed, he made up for with intensity and determination. Singletary, the youngest of ten children who grew up in a Houston ghetto, simply willed himself into becoming a great player and maintained his high level of play for 12 NFL seasons.

Singletary's aggressiveness fed off the intensity, drawing comparisons to another great Bears middle linebacker. "He plays like (Dick) Butkus did," said former Bears coach Mike Ditka. Former teammate Jim Osborne, a defensive tackle, seconded that notion. "I haven't seen a linebacker play with his intensity since I played with Butkus," he said.

What Singletary couldn't do when he joined the Bears, he quickly learned. He discovered ways to fight through blocks, he worked at covering backs on pass defense and he spent hours studying film and learning tendencies that would help him on the field. When he made a mistake, you could bet your life it would never happen again.

Nobody could match the work ethic and Singletary's desire to play at all times—and all costs. Over his 12 seasons, he missed only two games and once, when he noticed that the tip of one of his fingers was dangling by a thread of flesh, he had it taped and returned to the field.

But Singletary's influence was more than physical. The son of a preacher, he liked giving inspirational speeches to his teammates and continuously exhorted them to work harder. The Bears' hard work paid off with seven playoff appearances during Singletary's career and a victory in Super Bowl XX.

Singletary, who was named 1990 NFL Man of the Year for his off-field community service, made 10 Pro Bowl appearances before retiring after the 1992 season.

> "He looked right at me and said, 'Mr. Parmer, if you draft me, I'm going to be the best linebacker in the National Football League.' "
>
> FORMER BEARS SCOUT JIM PARMER

Midway Mayhem: Chicago linebacker Mike Singletary was the key to the Bears' famed 46 Defense which terrorized the NFL in their Super Bowl XX season.

Emmitt Smith

★★★★★ ## RUSHING ROULETTE

In retrospect, it seems incredible that 16 teams could have passed up Emmitt Smith in the 1990 National Football League draft. But then how can you explain destiny? The Dallas Cowboys enthusiastically grabbed the Florida running back with the 17th pick and laid the foundation for rapid reconstruction of a franchise.

Smith would fuel the Cowboys' rise with three consecutive rushing titles after a 937-yard rookie season. The Cowboys, who had finished 1-15 the year before his arrival, improved to 7-9 and 11-5 before dominating the NFL with consecutive Super Bowl championships after the 1992 and 1993 seasons and another after the 1995 campaign.

Did anybody envision such production from Smith, who left Florida with a year of eligibility remaining.

"Of course not, I'm no genius," said Cowboys running backs coach Joe Brodsky. "But if you look past the size, look past the fact that he's not as fast running straight down a track as you'd like a guy to be, you'd see a complete football player with magnificent strength in his thighs and hips."

That strength is used like a weapon by the no-nonsense Smith, who disdains the Barry Sanders-like jukes and fakes and runs through potential tacklers. He also has superb instincts that allow him to pick his holes, peripheral vision that Smith claims allows him to see both sidelines and the quickness to bolt to daylight. "He's the best north-south runner I've ever seen," said former Coach Jimmy Johnson, who directed the first two Super Bowl winners.

But the intangibles are what make Smith so special. Such as his fierce dedication to winning and his ability to play when most mortal men would prefer the sideline.

Smith was still competing with the Rams' Jerome Bettis for the 1993 rushing title when the Cowboys squared off with the New York Giants in a season finale that would decide the NFC East title. Midway through the game, he was tossed to the hard turf, separating his left shoulder. Smith was in terrible pain when Brodsky and Johnson told him to pack it in.

He refused. Smith carried 13 more times with the separated shoulder,

> ## "He's the best north-south runner I've ever seen."
>
> —FORMER DALLAS COACH JIMMY JOHNSON

the Cowboys won and he finished 57 yards ahead of Bettis. The inspired Cowboys went on to win the Super Bowl, with Smith earning MVP honors.

Smith ran for 1,484 yards in 1994, but both he and the Cowboys fell short in their title defenses. That wasn't the case in 1995 when he led the league with 1,773 yards and the Cowboys captured their third Super Bowl in four years.

Star of Texas: Emmitt Smith has become the mainstay of the Dallas Cowboys' running attack. He led the NFL in rushing three straight years from 1991 to 1993.

PERSONAL
BIRTHPLACE/DATE	Pensacola, Fla./5-15-69
HEIGHT/WEIGHT	5-9/209

AWARDS
PRO BOWL SELECTIONS	1990-95 seasons
SUPER BOWL MVP	XXVIII

CAREER
UNIVERSITY	Florida (left after 3 years)
DRAFT POSITION	1st Round (17th overall), Dallas, 1990
PRO TEAMS	6 Seasons, Dallas Cowboys (1990-95)

RUSHING, RECEIVING RECORD

	RUSHING				RECEIVING		
	ATT	YDS	AVG	TD	NO	YDS	TD
REGULAR SEASON	2,007	8,956	4.5	96	301	1,951	4
POSTSEASON	279	1,217	4.4	16	37	294	2

Lawrence Taylor

THE PROTOTYPE

PERSONAL
BIRTHPLACE/DATE   Williamsburg, Va / 2-4-59
HEIGHT/WEIGHT   6-3/243

AWARDS
PRO BOWL SELECTIONS   1981-90 seasons
SUPER BOWL MVP   None

CAREER
UNIVERSITY   North Carolina
DRAFT POSITION   1st Round (2nd overall), New York Giants, 1981
PRO TEAMS   13 Seasons, New York Giants (1981-93)
SACKS   Regular Season, 132.5, 2nd on all-time list. Postseason, 6.5.

He stood 6-feet-3, weighed 243 pounds and ran the field like a speedy wide receiver. It was a massive understatement to call Lawrence Taylor, with his menacing glare and riveting eyes, imposing.

His defensive presence made quarterbacks drop snaps, blockers jump offsides and coaches reconstruct game plans. When the New York Giants selected Taylor with the second overall pick of the 1981 draft, they turned loose a monster who would terrorize overmatched offensive coordinators for the next 13 seasons.

Taylor, more than anything, was the prototype outside linebacker. He dominated offensive linemen, chased down speedy running backs on the opposite side of the field and slammed quarterbacks to the turf like rag dolls, often fighting through triple-team blocks to reach them. In his rookie season, he earned defensive player of the year honors, an NFL first. By his second season, he already was the standard by which future outside linebackers would be judged.

"There are very few defensive players who can win a game by themselves," said television commentator John Madden, a former Raiders coach. "Lawrence Taylor is the most dominant defensive player I've seen... Taylor takes a game over by sheer force."

Former Philadelphia Eagles coach Dick Vermeil once called Taylor the most difficult player he ever coached against.

Not bad for a Williamsburg, Va, kid who didn't even play football until his third year of high school. After receiving consensus All-America honors as a senior at North Carolina, Taylor was sent off to search and destroy in the NFL wars.

> ## "Lawrence Taylor is the most dominant defensive player I've seen... Taylor takes a game over by sheer force."
>
> **TELEVISION COMMENTATOR JOHN MADDEN**

And the Giants, with big No 56 serving as their defensive anchor, stood tall after two decades of mediocrity. They qualified for the playoffs in 1981, 1984 and 1985 and won Super Bowls after the 1986 and 1990 seasons.

When he retired in January 1994, he ranked second on the all-time sacks list (132.5) and had collected ten Pro Bowl invitations.

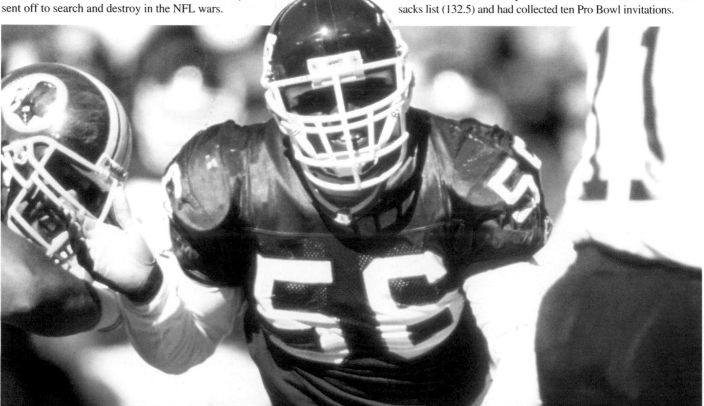

Redefining the position: New York Giants linebacker Lawrence Taylor set new standards for the way linebacking should be played.

Derrick Thomas

THE SACK MAN

PERSONAL	
BIRTHPLACE/DATE	Miami, Fla./1-1-67
HEIGHT/WEIGHT	6-3/240

AWARDS	
PRO BOWL SELECTIONS	1989-95 seasons
SUPER BOWL MVP	None

CAREER	
UNIVERSITY	Alabama
DRAFT POSITION	1st Round (4th overall), Kansas City, 1989
PRO TEAMS	7 Seasons, Kansas City Chiefs (1989-95)
SACKS	Regular Season, 85. Postseason, 7.5.

The essence of Derrick Thomas, football player, was captured in a 1990 game against the Seattle Seahawks. Double-teamed, triple-teamed and all but mugged several times by frustrated Seattle blockers, the Kansas City Chiefs outside linebacker still sacked quarterback Dave Krieg a startling seven times. Seven sacks, an NFL single-game record, is a pretty good season for most defensive players.

"He is undoubtedly one of the most gifted athletes there is," Seahawks tackle Andy Heck said after that game. "But don't forget, it wasn't just me he beat."

Since joining the Chiefs as the fourth overall pick of the 1989 draft, Thomas has been on a mission. He finished the 1995 season with 85 career sacks, more than any other player in that seven-year span. He has earned a reputation as the NFL's most dangerous pass rusher and offensive coordinators design special strategies to keep him in check.

"He is undoubtedly one of the most gifted athletes there is."

FORMER SEATTLE TACKLE ANDY HECK

Just like they did throughout the 1980s with New York Giants linebacker Lawrence Taylor, the man with whom Thomas is often compared.

"When a great linebacker came out of college," quarterback Billy Joe Tolliver once said, "people used to say, 'He's the next Lawrence Taylor.' Now they're saying, 'He's the next Derrick Thomas.'"

Indeed, Thomas looked like an "LT" clone when he came out of the University of Alabama after winning the 1988 Butkus Award as the nation's top collegiate linebacker. His 52 career sacks attracted a Chiefs coaching staff that wanted a big-play linebacker who could intimidate offenses and force turnovers.

Thomas was a perfect fit. A prototype linebacker at 6-feet-3, 240 pounds, he is strong enough to overpower blockers. But the key is his 4.58 speed and a starting burst that often puts him in the backfield before a lineman can get out of his stance. Thomas is so fast he can chase down speedy ballcarriers running to the opposite side and cover backs and tight ends on pass defense.

Thomas' passion, which has helped carry the Chiefs to six consecutive playoff appearances, also is evident off the field. The seven-time Pro Bowler has dedicated his life to various programs aiding the youth of Kansas City, a dedication that resulted in Thomas being named the 1993 NFL Man of the Year. He was one of three 1994 finalists for the Byron (Whizzer) White Humanitarian Award.

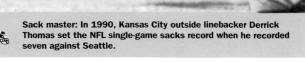

Sack master: In 1990, Kansas City outside linebacker Derrick Thomas set the NFL single-game sacks record when he recorded seven against Seattle.

Randy White

★★★★ DALLAS' MEAN MACHINE

PERSONAL

BIRTHPLACE/DATE	Wilmington, Del / 1-15-53
HEIGHT/WEIGHT	6-4/265

AWARDS

PRO BOWL SELECTIONS	1977-85 seasons
SUPER BOWL MVP	XII (co-MVP)

CAREER

UNIVERSITY	Maryland
DRAFT POSITION	1st Round (2nd overall), Dallas, 1975
PRO TEAMS	14 Seasons, Dallas Cowboys (1975-88)

When Randy White reported for the first time to the Dallas Cowboys training camp, safety Charlie Waters took one look at the rookie and dubbed him a "manster," as in half man, half monster. And for the next 14 National Football League seasons, White lived up to that billing as a Jekyll-Hyde personality in the body of a defensive tackle.

And what a body it was—6-foot-4, 265 pounds with gigantic arms to club overmatched blockers and the incredible strength to throw 300-pound linemen on their back. When running backs went to the opposite side of the field, as they often did, he used his 4.7 speed to chase them down.

"And he's mean," said long-time defensive partner Harvey Martin. "That's all you can say. He just gets up for games. Off the field, he's a nice guy, don't get me wrong. But he's mean otherwise."

Intense might be a better word. White was quiet, shy and soft-spoken off the field, easy to like. But once he put on the uniform, everything changed.

"You saw a very nice guy on the surface," former tackle Dave Stalls said. "But when you were around him all the time, you could see him change so fast. It was kind of amazing. He could be a pretty tough guy."

> "Off the field, he's a nice guy, don't get me wrong. But he's mean otherwise."

White, who won the Outland Trophy as college football's top lineman his senior season at Maryland, had to be tough. The right tackle slot he was being asked to fill once belonged to Bob Lilly, a Hall of Famer and a Cowboys legend. Dallas Coach Tom Landry first tried to convert his first-round draft pick to middle linebacker, but he finally gave up and moved him to tackle before the 1977 season.

The move paid quick dividends. With White consistently attracting double-teams, Martin became a pass-rushing demon from his end position. The Cowboys reached the Super Bowl and White and Martin shared sacks and MVP honors in a 27-10 victory over Denver. The Cowboys were back in the Super Bowl the next season, losing to Pittsburgh.

White continued his assault on NFL blockers through the 1988 season, earning nine Pro Bowl invitations and respect around the league as one of the game's all-time great defensive linemen. He was inducted into the Hall of Fame in 1994.

Power rusher: Randy White's career spanned 14 mainly successful seasons with the Dallas Cowboys, and the only coach he ever played for was Tom Landry.

★★★★★★★★★★★★

Reggie White

★★★ ## THE MINISTER OF DEFENSE

PERSONAL
BIRTHPLACE/DATE   Chattanooga, Tenn./12-19-61
HEIGHT/WEIGHT   6-5/295

AWARDS
PRO BOWL SELECTIONS   1986-95 seasons
SUPER BOWL MVP   None

CAREER
UNIVERSITY   Tennessee
DRAFT POSITION   1st Round (4th overall), Philadelphia, 1984 Supplemental Draft
PRO TEAMS   12 Seasons, Memphis USFL (1984-85); Philadelphia Eagles (1985-92); Green Bay Packers (1993-95)
SACKS   157, 1st on all-time list

On the field, Reggie White is a modern-day Rambo, dedicated to mayhem and destruction under the green-and-gold banner of the Green Bay Packers. Off the field, Reggie White is a humanitarian, an anti-drugs spokesman, an ordained minister dedicated to the destructive forces that prey on society.

Will the real Reggie White please stand up—all 6-feet-5, 295 pounds of him?

The Reggie White who prowls football fields on Sunday afternoons is the most dominant defensive end in the National Football League, one of the best ever to play. He dictates offensive strategy, shuts down running games, chases down ballcarriers with his sprinter speed and powers his way through double and triple-team blocks to terrorize quarterbacks.

"Reggie's the real deal," says Packers defensive line coach Larry Brooks. "His best qualities are his strength and his speed. And the bigger the game, the bigger he plays. When he gets to playing, it just shows—he's a force."

And a sack machine. Not counting the 23 1/2 he recorded in his first two professional seasons in the now-defunct United States Football League, White has 157 career sacks—more than any player in NFL history. And he constantly forces nervous quarterbacks to rush throws or scamper prematurely out of the pocket.

But White's biggest contribution might be the problems he creates for offensive coaches just by being on the field. For eight dominating seasons with the Philadelphia Eagles and three in Green Bay, White has attracted double and triple-team attention, freeing teammates to make big plays. In 1993, his first season with Green Bay, the Packers improved from a No. 23 defensive ranking to No. 2. When White left the Eagles in 1992, he became the most sought-after free agent in NFL history.

But the former University of Tennessee star has a "Dr. Jekyll" side to

"Reggie's the real deal."

his "Mr. Hyde." In 1992, the NFL Players Association named him winner of the prestigious Byron (Whizzer) White Humanitarian Award for service to team, community and country. He is involved in numerous charitable activities and regularly takes his ministry to churches and street corners. Although it's difficult to measure White's full impact on the Packers, coaches and fans point out that the team has qualified for the playoffs in each of his three seasons—after being shut out for a decade. White has been named to 10 Pro Bowl appearances and the only thing missing from his resume is a championship ring, a problem he almost corrected in 1995 when the Packers advanced to the NFC Championship Game.

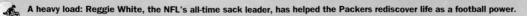
A heavy load: Reggie White, the NFL's all-time sack leader, has helped the Packers rediscover life as a football power.

Kellen Winslow

BETTER TO RECEIVE

PERSONAL
BIRTHPLACE/DATE   St Louis, Mo / 11-5-57
HEIGHT/WEIGHT   6-5/250

AWARDS
PRO BOWL SELECTIONS   1980-83, 1987 seasons
SUPER BOWL MVP   None

CAREER
UNIVERSITY   Missouri
DRAFT POSITION   1st Round (13th overall), San Diego, 1979
PRO TEAMS   9 Seasons, San Diego Chargers (1979-87)

RECEIVING RECORD

	No	Yds	Avg	Lg	TD
REGULAR SEASON	541	6,741	12.5	67t	45
POSTSEASON	28	380	13.6	33t	4

Kellen Winslow did not get the basic training that usually precedes Hall of Fame careers. But when he finally got his hands on a football, he wouldn't let go. Winslow, one of seven children raised by an East St Louis family, was not allowed to play football until his senior year in high school. His mother was afraid he would get hurt.

But her 6-foot-5, 250-pound son would make it through that season, four years at the University of Missouri and part of his rookie campaign with the San Diego Chargers before her fear would be warranted. And even the broken leg Winslow suffered in 1979 would be only a temporary setback.

When the Chargers grabbed Winslow with the 13th pick of the 1979 draft, they saw him as a perfect fit for an innovative, wide-open passing attack dubbed "Air-Coryell" in honor of Coach Don Coryell. Winslow, because of his size, deceptive speed and glue-like hands, was the final piece to the puzzle. He was the prototype tight end, the man who would re-define the position. He would be used like an extra wide receiver rather than in the traditional blocking and occasional receiving roles.

With Dan Fouts at quarterback, John Jefferson and Charlie Joiner at wide receiver and Winslow at tight end, the Chargers were virtually unstoppable. In 1980, Jefferson, Joiner and Winslow became the first trio in NFL history to catch passes for more than 100 yards in a game and 1,000 yards in a season. Winslow, working his magic over the middle like no one before him, led the league in catches in 1980 (89) and 1981 (88).

He tied an NFL record in 1981 by catching five touchdown passes in a game with the Raiders and helped the Chargers reach the AFC Championship Game after the 1980 and 1981 seasons.

"Kellen Winslow was the finest tight end ever to play football and one of the most dominant players of his era," Fouts said. "You could put the ball anywhere and you knew he'd come up with it."

Winslow made four consecutive Pro Bowl appearances before a career-threatening knee injury sidelined him in 1984. Defying odds, he made the painful journey through rehabilitation and earned another Pro Bowl citation in 1987 before ending his career with 541 catches for 6,741 yards.

"You could put the ball anywhere and you knew he'd come up with it."

FORMER SAN DIEGO QUARTERBACK DAN FOUTS

Tightly charged: San Diego's All-Pro tight end Kellen Winslow (80) cuts between San Francisco defensive backs Dwight Hicks (22) and Ronnie Lott (42).

Steve Young

OUT OF THE SHADOW

From his college days as a record-setting quarterback at Brigham Young University to that 1991 season when he officially became Joe Montana's successor as quarterback of the 49ers, Steve Young had been trapped in no-win situations.

First as quarterback of the Los Angeles Express of the dying United States Football League, then as quarterback of the NFL's lowly Tampa Bay Buccaneers. Even when Young was traded to San Francisco in 1987, he watched from the bench as Montana directed the 49ers to Super Bowl victories after the 1988 and '89 seasons.

When he finally got his chance in 1991, Young found that his battle against Montana's legacy and fan expectations was more difficult than the weekly skirmishes on the field. The only way to survive, he finally decided, was to be himself.

When Young is "being himself," opposing defenses are in trouble. His rifle left arm is selective and accurate. When he can't find a Jerry Rice or John Taylor open downfield, he tucks the ball under his arm and sprints for big yardage. If Young is not the best scrambling quarterback in football history, he's close. And he complements his physical abilities with intelligence, resourcefulness, modesty and a willingness to spread credit for his team's success.

Finally armed and dangerous, Young proceeded to win an unprecedented four consecutive passing titles, firing 106 touchdown passes and running for 17 more. When he finished the 1994 regular season, he was the highest rated passer in NFL history (96.8).

But that was not enough. Young finally punched a hole in Montana's massive shadow in Super Bowl XXIX when he fired a Super Bowl-record six touchdown passes in the 49ers' 49-26 victory over San Diego, one more than Montana had thrown in Super Bowl XXIV against Denver. He also won MVP honors and the 49ers won their record fifth championship. "For him to come through under that

"The 1990s belong to Steve Young and he deserves that moment."

49ERS PRESIDENT CARMEN POLICY

kind of pressure, was amazing," said former 49ers wide receiver Dwight Clark.

President Carmen Policy puts Young's accomplishments into perspective.

"Joe was a huge part of what made the 49ers great," he said. "He is the 1980s and that should be unblemished and untarnished. By the same token, the 1990s belongs to Steve Young and he deserves that moment unblemished and untarnished."

No drop off: Steve Young replaced the legendary Joe Montana as San Francisco's quarterback and won four consecutive NFL passing titles.

PERSONAL

BIRTHPLACE/DATE	Salt Lake City, Utah/10-11-61
HEIGHT/WEIGHT	6-2/205

AWARDS

PRO BOWL SELECTIONS	1992-95 seasons
SUPER BOWL MVP	XXIX

CAREER

UNIVERSITY	Brigham Young
DRAFT POSITION	1st Round (1st overall), Tampa Bay, 1984 Supplemental Draft
PRO TEAMS	13 Seasons, Los Angeles, USFL (1984-85); Tampa Bay Buccaneers (1985-86); San Francisco 49ers (1987-95)

PASSING, RUSHING RECORD

	PASSING					
	ATT.	COMP	YDS	PCT	INT	TD
REGULAR SEASON	2,876	1,845	23,069	.642	79	160
POSTSEASON	308	191	2,212	.620	7	14

	RUSHING			
	ATT	YDS	AVG	TD
REGULAR SEASON	539	3,219	6.0	30
POSTSEASON	69	444	6.4	6

A Super Way to End Every

★★★★★★★★★★★★★★★★★★★★★★★★★★★★★★★★★★★★★

It's a media monster, a celebration, a near religious experience. For one super Sunday in January, the entire world stops to watch football. It's called the Super Bowl and it has become the most anticipated sports event of the year.

It wasn't always so Super. When the Kansas City Chiefs and Green Bay Packers squared off in January 1967, reducing football's seven-year war to a bragging-rights battle that finally would produce a clear-cut winner, it was dubbed the "AFL-NFL World Championship Game." Officially.

Unofficially, a more colorful name was circulating through the press box at Los Angeles' Memorial Coliseum, courtesy of Kansas City owner and American Football League founder Lamar Hunt. As the story goes, Hunt was inspired one day by the name "Super Ball," a bouncy rubber ball that his children played with. In a meeting to work on details for the championship game, he referred to it as the "Super Bowl," and it caught on in private and then in public.

Skeptical just how "super" this annual series was going to be, the NFL deferred on Hunt's colorful new name. The skepticism was short-lived. After the powerful Packers had dominated the Chiefs and Oakland Raiders in the first two title games, Joe Namath and the New York Jets pumped life into the AFL-NFL feud in 1969 when they deflated the powerful Baltimore Colts and the Chiefs followed suit a year later by dismantling Minnesota's supposedly invincible machine. Hunt's "Super Bowl" was here to stay.

The idea of an inter-league championship game was but a hazy fantasy in 1959 when Hunt, a Texas oilman who had been thwarted in his attempts to bring an NFL franchise to Dallas, began piecing together an ownership puzzle that would become the AFL. The NFL had fought this kind of war before, but not against Lamar Hunt and his band of deep-pocketed associates.

When the NFL located a new franchise in Dallas and succeeded in running Hunt out of his own backyard, he simply took his Dallas Texans' AFL team to Kansas City in 1963. From 1960 to 1966, a costly war was waged for players and respect—and the all-important television contracts. When the AFL signed a $36-million, five-year deal with NBC-TV in 1964, guaranteeing its perseverance at least through the decade, the rival leagues were motivated to begin serious peace talks that would lead to a 1966 merger agreement.

Although the AFL and NFL would not merge under a common banner until 1970, the agreement did set up a common draft and a yearly AFL-NFL championship game that would begin after the 1966 season.

Most of the 61,946 fans who showed up January 15, 1967, at the Coliseum (only two-thirds of capacity), and the 60 million-plus who watched on the simultaneous CBS and NBC broadcasts viewed the Packers-Chiefs inaugural as a curiosity piece. The question was not who would win, but by how much. The answer was 35-10 and NFL fans smugly said, "I told you so."

It was more of the same the following year when Vince Lombardi's Packers routed the Raiders. But little did anybody know that the Packers simply were setting the stage for Namath, who would almost single-handedly change curiosity to passion and give personality to an event that would never be lacking for that quality again.

 Crimson tide: Super Bowl III MVP Joe Namath attended the University of Alabama, as did the MVP in Super Bowls I and II, Bart Starr.

Season

★★★★★★ THE SUPER BOWL

The colorful, flamboyant Namath strutted and pranced around Miami in the week preceding Super Bowl III, guaranteeing a Jets victory over the powerful Colts and expounding on the superior talents of AFL quarterbacks. His behavior was outlandish, his victory prediction illogical. The Colts were listed as 18-point favorites.

But when Namath and the Jets delivered a 16-7 victory, the football establishment was shocked. And when the Chiefs followed by beating the Vikings, the AFL took its place as a football equal. Super Bowl V would be the first under a common umbrella.

The Super Bowl, which is played two weeks after the conference championship games, has grown from that humble beginning into a media celebration. Super Bowl XXX was televised into 187 countries and territories with an estimated worldwide audience of 800 million.

By kickoff, everybody is well-versed on the teams and the players.

Critics who point out that the Super Bowl has been burdened by one-sided mismatches can't deny it also has been blessed by many outstanding individual performances. Quarterbacks like Bart Starr, Joe Namath, Jim Plunkett, Doug Williams, Terry Bradshaw, Troy Aikman, Larry Csonka, Franco Harris, Joe Montana, and Steve Young have written personal legacies that will be difficult to top. So have running backs like John Riggins, Timmy Smith, Tony Dorsett, Marcus Allen and Emmitt Smith and receivers like Max McGee, Jerry Rice, Lynn Swann, and John Stallworth.

But the most lasting legacy belongs to Lombardi, whose name is imprinted on the Super Bowl Trophy—the symbol for what has become the greatest show on earth.

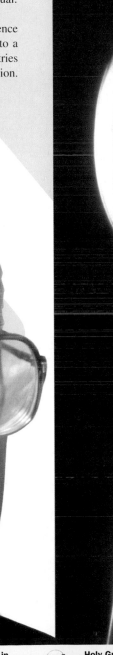

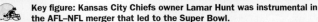

Key figure: Kansas City Chiefs owner Lamar Hunt was instrumental in the AFL–NFL merger that led to the Super Bowl.

Holy Grail: The Lombardi Trophy, given annually to the Super Bowl winner, is what all 30 NFL teams dream of collecting at season start.

First World Championship Game AFL vs NFL

TM/©1966 NFL

Jan 15, 1967, at the Los Angeles Coliseum
PACKERS 35, CHIEFS 10

★★★★★★★★★★★★★★★★★★

SCORING SUMMARY

KANSAS CITY	0	10	0	0—10
GREEN BAY	7	7	14	7—35

GB	McGee 37 pass from Starr (Chandler kick)
KC	McClinton 7 pass from Dawson (Mercer kick)
GB	Taylor 14 run (Chandler kick)
KC	FG Mercer 31
GB	Pitts 5 run (Chandler kick)
GB	McGee 13 pass from Starr (Chandler kick)
GB	Pitts 1 run (Chandler kick)

 Super charged: Green Bay's Max McGee races to the end zone to score the first touchdown in Super Bowl history.

After seven years of bitter hostilities, the AFL-NFL war was fought head-to-head, mano a' mano for the first time amid the glitz and hoopla of television cameras, blaring bands and skyward-rising pigeons.

Most of the 60-million-plus television viewers and 61,946 fans at the Los Angeles Coliseum were drawn more by curiosity than expectations of a competitive championship game. How could the 7-year-old Chiefs possibly compete with Vince Lombardi's noble and powerful Packers, who would be carrying the 47-year-old banner of the NFL? Judging by the final score, they couldn't.

But that score was deceiving. Throughout a competitive first half, quarterbacks Bart Starr and Len Dawson battled on even terms and the Packers carried only a 14-10 lead into halftime. Green Bay scored on Starr's 37-yard touchdown pass to Max McGee and Jim Taylor's 14-yard run. The Chiefs countered with Dawson's seven-yard pass to Curtis McClinton and Mike Mercer's 31-yard field goal.

The game's turning point might have come in the locker room when Lombardi, hoping to pressure Dawson, ordered his defense to blitz. Early in the second half, Dawson, under pressure, wobbled a pass toward the sideline that Packers safety Willie Wood picked off and returned 50 yards to the 5. Elijah Pitts scored on the next play for a 21-10 lead and the Packers were off to the races.

Starr, who completed 16 of 23 passes for 250 yards to earn MVP honors, added a 13-yard TD pass to McGee, and Pitts ran one yard for a fourth-quarter touchdown to complete the scoring. The Green Bay defense harried Dawson into a 5-for-12 second-half performance that doomed the Chiefs.

The NFL's football crown was safe for at least another year.

SUPER BOWL II

JAN 14, 1968, AT THE ORANGE BOWL, MIAMI
PACKERS 33, RAIDERS 14

★★★★★★★★★★★★★★★★★★★

The Packers, playing inspired football in what they suspected would be Vince Lombardi's last game as Green Bay coach, blitzed the overmatched Raiders early and proudly carried the NFL banner to their fifth championship of the decade.

With quarterback Bart Starr performing flawlessly en route to his second straight MVP citation and Don Chandler kicking four field goals, the Packers were never challenged. Starr's public dissection of Oakland's defense was viewed by 75,546 reverential fans at Miami's Orange Bowl.

SCORING SUMMARY

	1	2	3	4	
GREEN BAY	3	13	10	7	—33
OAKLAND	0	7	0	7	—14

GB	FG Chandler 39
GB	FG Chandler 20
GB	Dowler 62 pass from Starr (Chandler kick)
OAK	Miller 23 pass from Lamonica (Blanda kick)
GB	FG Chandler 43
GB	Anderson 2 run (Chandler kick)
GB	FG Chandler 31
GB	Adderley 60 interception return (Chandler kick)
OAK	Miller 23 pass from Lamonica (Blanda kick)

The Packers didn't waste any time, scoring on their first three possessions. Chandler kicked two field goals to open the scoring and Starr made it 13-0 when he picked up a Raiders blitz and fired a stunning 62-yard bomb to Boyd Dowler. After the Raiders cut the margin with a 23-yard Daryle Lamonica-to-Bill Miller touchdown pass, Chandler kicked a 43-yard field goal for a 16-7 halftime lead.

Things only got worse for the Raiders. Donny Anderson's two-yard third-quarter run and Chandler's 31-yard field goal lifted the lead to 26-7 and set up cornerback Herb Adderley for the coup de grace. In the fourth quarter, Adderley picked off a pass by Lomonica, followed crunching blocks by defensive tackles Henry Jordan and Ron Kostelnik and raced 60 yards for a touchdown. Another 23-yard Lamonica-to-Miller TD pass was too little, too late.

The game, which drew football's first $3-million gate, indeed was Lombardi's last as Green Bay coach and marked the end of a great dynasty.

PACKERS ICE COWBOYS

It was decision time. Quarterback Bart Starr and Coach Vince Lombardi discussed strategy on the Green Bay sideline with the 1967 NFL championship riding on the next play. The Packers, trailing 17-14, were 2 feet away from their third straight crown and fifth in seven seasons. They also were 16 seconds away from defeat.

The scene was frozen Lambeau Field in Green Bay and 50,861 shivering fans watched in anticipation. The next play would decide the "Ice Bowl," a game played in 13-below-zero temperatures with a stiff wind making it feel more like minus-35.

Starr returned to the Green Bay huddle and relayed the decision to his teammates. There would be no field-goal attempt. They would gamble. Lombardi and Starr had agreed on a quarterback sneak, although, in the huddle, Starr called for a handoff to fullback Chuck Mercein.

But Starr took the snap, followed guard Jerry Kramer and dove into the end zone, completing the 68-yard drive. Packers 21, Cowboys 17. Green Bay would represent the NFL in Super Bowl II.

Starr's gamble ended a dramatic test of nerves and endurance. After Green Bay had taken a 14-0 lead on two Starr TD passes to Boyd Dowler, the Cowboys had fought back to take a fourth-quarter lead on Danny Reeves' 50-yard halfback pass to Lance Rentzel.

Repeating the dose: Green Bay quarterback Bart Starr was named MVP in Super Bowls I and II. He's now in the Pro Football Hall of Fame.

SUPER BOWL III

JAN 12, 1969, AT THE ORANGE BOWL, MIAMI
JETS 16, COLTS 7

★★★★★★★★★★★★★★★★

The AFL was badly in need of a savior after two lopsided World Championship Game defeats. What it got was a brash victory prediction from a young New York Jets quarterback. "We're going to win on Sunday, I guarantee it," announced Joe Namath when he appeared before the Miami Touchdown Club on the Thursday before the game. Those amazing words circulated quickly and twice-humiliated AFL officials cringed. Namath's guarantee probably would have an inspirational effect on the powerful, once-beaten Colts (15-1 overall), who already were listed as 18-point favorites.

That appeared to be the case as the Colts moved to the New York 19-yard line early in the opening quarter. But Lou Michaels missed a 27-yard field goal. Again the Colts threatened after recovering a fumble at the Jets 12. But an Earl Morrall pass was picked off by Randy Beverly in the end zone, one of three first-half interceptions Morrall would throw. Suddenly, the momentum shifted.

Namath's passing and the power running of Matt Snell moved the Jets into scoring position midway through the second quarter and Snell's four-yard TD run gave them a 7-0 halftime lead.

The fired-up New York defense smothered the bewildered Colts in the second half. It forced a first-possession fumble that set up Jim Turner's 32-yard field goal and Namath, who would earn MVP honors for his 206-yard passing performance, moved his team in position for two more Turner field goals.

Only a late Johnny Unitas-led drive that resulted in a one-yard Jerry Hill touchdown run kept Baltimore from being shut out. The Colts, badly outplayed and humiliated, watched in disbelief as Namath walked off the field after the game, his forefinger held high signaling the obvious.

The Jets, and the AFL, were No 1 and the new league had its savior—as well as a large dose of respectability.

SCORING SUMMARY

NY JETS	0	7	6	3—16
BALTIMORE	0	0	0	7—7

Keeping his promise: Joe Namath delivered on his guarantee that the New York Jets would defeat the heavily-favored Baltimore Colts in Super Bowl III.

SUPER BOWL IV

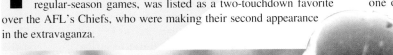

JAN 11, 1970, AT TULANE STADIUM, NEW ORLEANS
CHIEFS 23, VIKINGS 7

★★★★★★★★★★★★★★

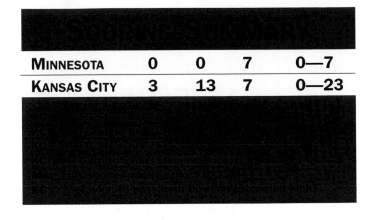

				SCORING SUMMARY	
MINNESOTA	0	0	7	0—7	
KANSAS CITY	3	13	7	0—23	

The NFL, anxious to avenge the indignation suffered by the Colts, sent another powerful representative into the fourth edition of the Super Bowl. Minnesota, which had lost only two regular-season games, was listed as a two-touchdown favorite over the AFL's Chiefs, who were making their second appearance in the extravaganza.

Not only did the Chiefs have to contend with the Vikings' quick-strike offense and rugged defensive line dubbed "The Purple People Eaters," they had to do so under a cloud of suspicion. In the week preceding the game, Chiefs quarterback Len Dawson was named as one of several players who would be called to testify in a federal investigation into sports gambling.

Dawson, who later was cleared of any wrong-doing, was devastated by the reports. Players and coaches were angered by the timing. It was a distraction that could have killed what little chance the Chiefs were given of pulling an upset.

But it didn't. The Chiefs, confident and surprisingly ready to play, dramatically turned the tables on the Vikings and gave the AFL its second straight Super Bowl upset, tying the young series at two games apiece.

Utilizing Dawson's short, precision passing and a defense that stuffed Minnesota's powerful running game, the Chiefs methodically dominated the game. Three Jan Stenerud field goals opened the scoring and Mike Garrett's five-yard second-quarter run gave Kansas City a 16-0 halftime lead.

Dave Osborn's four-yard third-quarter TD run gave the Vikings temporary hope, but Dawson and wide receiver Otis Taylor took care of that on the Chiefs' next possession. Dawson fired a six-yard out pattern to Taylor, who broke two tackles and raced a total of 46 yards for the clinching touchdown.

Minnesota's futility was dramatized in the fourth period when quarterback Joe Kapp, battered and injured, had to be helped off the field after being sacked. There was no such exit for Dawson, who walked off the field a conquering hero.

★★★★★★★★★★

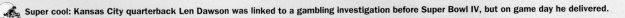
Super cool: Kansas City quarterback Len Dawson was linked to a gambling investigation before Super Bowl IV, but on game day he delivered.

SUPER BOWL V

JAN 17, 1971, AT THE ORANGE BOWL, MIAMI
COLTS 16, COWBOYS 13

★★★★★★★★★★★★★★★

This was both the worst and the best of the Super Bowls to date. The worst: The teams combined for 11 turnovers in a penalty-filled contest that neither team appeared capable of winning. The best: Baltimore's Jim O'Brien kicked a 32-yard field goal with five seconds remaining, ending the tightest of the five Super Bowls on an exciting note.

This was the first Super Bowl featuring teams under the single NFL banner. Baltimore represented the new American Conference, Dallas the National Conference. It was played before 79,204 fans at Miami's Orange Bowl.

The comedy of errors started early when Ron Gardin fumbled a punt return (the first of seven Colts turnovers) and the Cowboys converted it into Mike Clark's 14-yard field goal. Clark's 30-yard kick made it 6-0 in the second quarter.

But the Colts struck back when a Johnny Unitas pass was deflected to tight end John Mackey, who ran the rest of the way for a 75-yard touchdown pass play. O'Brien's conversion kick was blocked, leaving the game tied. Dallas regained the lead in the second quarter on Craig Morton's seven-yard touchdown pass to Duane Thomas.

The game's key play occurred early in the second half when Dallas drove to the Baltimore 2-yard line, only to lose the ball on a Thomas fumble. Another turnover, Rich Volk's interception of a Morton pass, set up Baltimore's tying touchdown, a two-yard run by Tom Nowatzke.

O'Brien's game winner was set up by a Mike Curtis interception.

Last kick drama: Baltimore won Super Bowl V when rookie Jim O'Brien's kick with five seconds remaining sailed through the uprights from 32 yards away.

SUPER BOWL VI

JAN 16, 1972, AT TULANE STADIUM, NEW ORLEANS
COWBOYS 24, DOLPHINS 3

★★★★★★★★★★★★★★

SCORING SUMMARY

DALLAS	3	7	7	7—24
MIAMI	0	3	0	0—3

Dal — FG Clark 9.
Dal — Alworth 7 pass from Staubach (Clark kick).
Mia — FG Yepremian 31.
Dal — D. Thomas 3 run (Clark kick).
Dal — Ditka 7 pass from Staubach (Clark kick).

The Cowboys, who had fumbled and bumbled their way through Super Bowl V, were much more efficient against the young Dolphins. Dominating both the offensive and defensive lines, they rushed for a Super Bowl-record 252 yards while holding Miami to 185 total yards and no touchdowns.

It wasn't pretty, but it was effective. The Cowboys jumped on top in the opening quarter when Miami fullback Larry Csonka, who had not fumbled all season, lost control of the ball near midfield, setting up a nine-yard Mike Clark field goal.

Dallas added to its lead in the second quarter when Roger Staubach, who completed 12 of 19 passes en route to MVP honors, culminated a 76-yard drive with a seven-yard TD toss to Lance Alworth. That was all the Cowboys would need.

Garo Yepremian gave the Dolphins brief hope when he drilled a 31-yard field goal just before halftime, but the Cowboys would regain control on their first possession of the second half. With Duane Thomas doing most of the damage against the tiring Miami defense, the Cowboys powered the ball 71 yards and scored on Thomas' three-yard run for a 17-3 lead. Staubach's seven-yard fourth-quarter TD strike to tight end Mike Ditka closed out the scoring.

Thomas rushed for a game-high 95 yards, atoning for his untimely fumble against Baltimore in Super Bowl V. The Cowboys did some atoning of their own and silenced critics who said they couldn't win the big game. Dallas had lost to the Packers in the 1966 and 1967 NFL Championship Games before losing to the Colts in Super Bowl V.

 Big rush: Duane Thomas' third-quarter touchdown run helped the Cowboys pull away en route to victory in Super Bowl VI.

SUPER BOWL VII

JAN 14, 1973, AT THE LOS ANGELES COLISEUM
DOLPHINS 14, REDSKINS 7

★★★★★★★★★★★★★★★★

SCORING SUMMARY

MIAMI	7	7	0	0—14
WASHINGTON	0	0	0	7—7

It appeared Miami's "No-Name Defense" would write the perfect ending to the Dolphins' perfect season. It had stuffed, throttled and denied the Redskins for more than three quarters and was on the verge of posting the first shutout in Super Bowl history.

But fate would not let that script play out. With Coach Don Shula's Dolphins leading 14-0 and about to put the wraps on the first undefeated, untied season in the NFL's 53-year history, little placekicker Garo Yepremian lined up for a 42-yard field goal attempt that everybody thought would clinch the Dolphins' date with destiny.

But when Yepremian kicked the ball squarely into defensive lineman Bill Brundige, it deflected back, took a big hop and landed in his arms. Instead of falling on the ball, Yepremian saw several massive bodies charging toward him and desperately tried to heave it forward. The ball slipped out of his hand to cornerback Mike Bass, who grabbed it and ran 49 yards for a touchdown with 2:07 remaining.

With the shoutout gone and the victory no longer secure, the Dolphins were forced to hunker down one more time. Washington regained possession with 1:14 remaining and the Miami defense swarmed Redskins quarterback Billy Kilmer, ending the game, fittingly, with a nine-yard sack.

The victory, Miami's record-setting 17th, was accomplished like most of its other 16—efficiently. With an offense featuring the three-pronged running attack of Larry Csonka, Jim Kiick and Mercury

Morris and quarterback Bob Griese directing a controlled passing game, the Dolphins were usually in command.

They jumped on the Redskins in the opening quarter when Griese connected with Howard Twilley on a 28-yard touchdown pass and extended the lead to 14-0 on Kiick's one-yard second-quarter run. The rest of the game belonged to the defense.

Csonka picked up a clock-killing 112 yards for Miami, but MVP honors went to safety Jake Scott, who picked off two passes—one a drive-killer in the Miami end zone.

 Big play: Miami's Jake Scott had two interceptions, this one in the end zone.

THE IMMACULATE RECEPTION

The young, defensive Steelers, playing in only the franchise's second playoff game, were looking for respect. What they got was a miracle.

It appeared the Steelers' playoff adventure would be short when Oakland quarterback Ken Stabler, a fourth-quarter replacement for ineffective starter Daryle Lamonica, scrambled 30 yards for a touchdown with 1:13 remaining in a 1972 AFC divisional-round battle. Stabler's run capped an 80-yard drive and gave the Raiders their first lead of the day, 7-6.

The Steelers were in trouble. Quarterback Terry Bradshaw, trying to get them in field-goal position, completed two short passes to the Pittsburgh 40-yard line before missing on three in a row. Facing a fourth down with 22 seconds remaining, Bradshaw avoided heavy pressure, then spotted Frenchy Fuqua streaking downfield and fired the ball.

Raiders defensive back Jack Tatum reached Fuqua at the same moment as the ball and the ball bounced backward off one or both of them, apparently ending the threat. But just before the ball hit the turf at the Oakland 42, Pittsburgh running back Franco Harris, running full speed, reached down, grabbed the ball off his shoetops and raced toward the goal line.

Harris fought off a desperation shove from defender Jimmy Warren and scored standing up—with five seconds remaining. Final score: Steelers 13, Raiders 7.

SUPER BOWL VIII

TM/©1973 NFL

JAN 13, 1974, AT RICE STADIUM, HOUSTON
DOLPHINS 24, VIKINGS 7

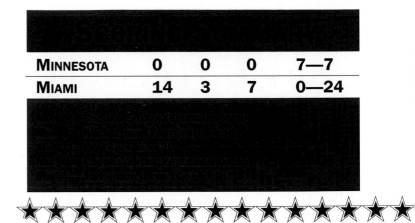

MINNESOTA	0	0	0	7—7
MIAMI	14	3	7	0—24

It wasn't the end to a perfect season, but Don Shula's Dolphins became only the second team to win consecutive Super Bowls. And nobody in the professional football world would deny that this team was just as dominant as the oh-so-perfect Dolphins of 1973.

This Super Bowl was a mismatch from the opening kickoff. It pitted a Minnesota run defense that ranked 23rd during the regular season against a relentless Miami ground attack. The Dolphins wasted little time probing the Vikings' weakness, putting together consecutive 62 and 56-yard touchdown drives while controlling the ball for 11 minutes of the opening quarter.

The first touchdown was scored by bulldozing fullback Larry Csonka, who would add a third-quarter TD and finish his MVP outing with a Super Bowl-record 145 yards. Csonka's five-yard run and Jim Kiick's one-yarder gave the Dolphins a 14-0 lead before the Vikings even managed a first down.

A 28-yard Garo Yepremian field goal increased the margin to 17-0 before halftime and Csonka's two-yard third-quarter run made the score 24-0 before Vikings quarterback Fran Tarkenton broke the shutout with a four-yard fourth-quarter run.

The victory, which was forged before 71,882 fans at Houston's Rice Stadium, lifted the Dolphins' final record to 15-2 and their two-season mark to 32-2—the best back-to-back finishes in NFL history. Only the 1966 and 1967 Green Bay Packers had won back-to-back Super Bowls. Conversely, the Vikings became the first team to lose two Super Bowls.

 **Minnesota Csonked:** Larry Csonka scored two touchdowns in Super Bowl VIII as the Miami Dolphins won their second straight Super Bowl, defeating the Vikings 24-7.

SUPER BOWL IX

TM/©1974 NFL

JAN 12, 1975, AT TULANE STADIUM, NEW ORLEANS

STEELERS 16, VIKINGS 6

★★★★★★★★★★★★★★★★

A new team crashed the Super Bowl party, but its patriarch was a familiar face in football circles. Pittsburgh's Art Rooney, who founded the team in 1933, had been waiting 42 years for his first championship

The Steelers of Coach Chuck Noll gave it to him. Competing against a Vikings team that was looking for its first Super Bowl victory after two losses, Noll had twin weapons at his disposal—a smothering, "Steel Curtain" defense and running back Franco Harris. The Vikings were in trouble.

Neither team could get untracked in a defensive first half that ended with the unlikely score of 2-0. Pittsburgh scored a safety when Fran Tarkenton's handoff hit running back Dave Osborn on the hip, and the ball bounded into the Minnesota end zone, where Tarkenton fell on it. He was touched down by Pittsburgh end Dwight White for a safety.

Minnesota made its second critical mistake when Bill Brown took the second-half kickoff, returned it two yards and fumbled, setting up Pittsburgh on the Vikings' 30-yard line. Four plays later, Harris swept left end for nine yards and a touchdown.

The Vikings finally broke through in the fourth quarter when Matt Blair blocked a Bobby Walden punt and Terry Brown recovered in the end zone. But Steelers quarterback Terry Bradshaw answered with a clock-eating 66-yard drive that culminated with a four-yard, game-sealing TD pass to Larry Brown.

Harris, who was named MVP, ran for a Super Bowl-record 158 yards. The Steelers defense, led by tackle Mean Joe Greene, linebackers Jack Lambert and Jack Ham and cornerback Mel Blount, held the Vikings to 119 total yards, 17 on the ground, and intercepted three passes.

Big play: A four-yard touchdown reception by Pittsburgh's Larry Brown (87) insured the Steelers' first Super Bowl victory and Minnesota's second straight loss.

SUPER BOWL X

JAN 18, 1976, AT THE ORANGE BOWL, MIAMI
STEELERS 21, COWBOYS 17

The "Steel Curtain" continued to shroud the NFL, but Cowboys quarterback Roger Staubach did manage to poke a few holes in it. When all was said and done, however, the Steelers had given long-suffering Pittsburgh fans their second consecutive championship.

The Cowboys sent a quick message that it would not be easy—a 29-yard touchdown pass from Staubach to Drew Pearson one play after a fumbled punt attempt on Pittsburgh's first offensive series. It marked the first time all season the Steelers had surrendered first-quarter points.

It didn't take Pittsburgh long to get them back. Quarterback Terry Bradshaw moved the Steelers 67 yards on their next possession, a drive that ended with a seven-yard touchdown pass to Randy Grossman. The Steelers fell behind again in the second quarter on a 36-yard field goal by Dallas' Toni Fritsch.

The Cowboys maintained their 10-7 advantage until the Steelers struck for 14 fourth-quarter points on an unusual scoring combination—a safety, two Roy Gerela field goals and a 64-yard Bradshaw bomb to Lynn Swann. Pittsburgh led 21-10 with 3:02 left to play.

But Staubach was not finished. He quickly moved the Cowboys 80 yards, completing the drive with a 34-yard TD pass to Percy Howard. Then, after the Steelers were forced to give the ball up on downs with 1:22 remaining, he moved the Cowboys to the Pittsburgh 38 before throwing a goal-line pass that was picked off by Steelers safety Glen Edwards.

Pittsburgh's Swann, who caught four passes for 161 yards, was named MVP.

SCORING SUMMARY

DALLAS	7	3	0	7—17
PITTSBURGH	7	0	0	14—21

DAL	D. Pearson 29 pass from Staubach (Fritsch kick)
PIT	Grossman 7 pass from Bradshaw (Gerela kick)
DAL	FG Fritsch 36
PIT	Safety, Harrison blocked Hoopes' punt through end zone
PIT	FG Gerela 36
PIT	FG Gerela 18
PIT	Swann 64 pass from Bradshaw (kick failed)
DAL	P. Howard 34 pass from Staubach (Fritsch kick)

Graceful Swann: This falling 53-yard catch by Lynn Swann was one of four for 161 yards by the Pittsburgh receiver, who was the game's MVP.

ROGER SAYS HAIL MARY

Dallas quarterback Roger Staubach had been in desperate situations before. He knew this one called for extraordinary measures.

"I guess it's a 'Hail Mary' pass," he said after firing a 50-yard touchdown bomb to Drew Pearson, giving the Cowboys an unlikely 17-14 victory over Minnesota in a 1975 NFC Divisional playoff game. "You throw it up and pray he catches it."

Staubach and the Cowboys had been thwarted all day by the Vikings' Purple People Eaters defense and fell behind, 14-10, when Minnesota's Brent McClanahan ran one yard for a touchdown with 5:24 remaining.

With less than a minute left and facing fourth down on his own 25-yard line, Staubach bought new life for Dallas with a 25-yard pass to Pearson. But with 32 seconds remaining, the Cowboys decided it was time to go for broke.

Staubach heaved the second-and-10 pass toward the end zone, again looking for Pearson. But this time the pass was underthrown and Pearson came out of the end zone for the ball. He snatched it away from defenders Nate Wright and Terry Brown and rolled into the end zone with 24 seconds remaining.

Vikings players and Coach Bud Grant screamed for offensive pass interference as the stunned Minnesota crowd watched in disbelief. The touchdown stood.

SUPER BOWL XI

JAN 9, 1977, AT THE ROSE BOWL, PASADENA, CAL
RAIDERS 32, VIKINGS 14

★★★★★★★★★★★★★★

SCORING SUMMARY

OAKLAND	0	16	3	13—32
MINNESOTA	0	0	7	7—14

OAK	FG Mann 24
OAK	Casper 1 pass from Stabler (Mann kick)
OAK	Banaszak 1 run (kick failed)
OAK	FG Mann 40
MIN	S. White 8 pass from Tarkenton (Cox kick)
OAK	Banaszak 2 run (Mann kick)
OAK	Brown 75 interception return (kick failed)
MIN	Voigt 13 pass from Lee (Cox kick)

Nine years after getting flogged by Green Bay in Super Bowl II, the Raiders claimed football's biggest prize. But their victory was obscured by the shadow of Minnesota's futility—a record four Super Bowl losses in eight years.

The Vikings, seeking redemption under the close scrutiny of 81 million television viewers and 103,438 fans at the Rose Bowl in Pasadena, Cal, got a first-quarter break when Fred McNeill blocked a Ray Guy punt and recovered at the Oakland 3-yard line. But on a second-down play, Brent McClanahan fumbled, Oakland's Willie Hall recovered and momentum shifted dramatically.

Quarterback Ken Stabler quickly drove the Raiders 90 yards to an Errol Mann field goal. Two more second-quarter possessions produced a one-yard Stabler-to-Dave Casper touchdown pass and a one-yard Pete Banaszak TD run. Not only had the Raiders jumped to a 16-0 halftime lead, they had dominated the Vikings: 16-4 in first downs, 288-86 in total yards, 166-27 in rushing yards and 122-59 in passing yards.

The Vikings were better in the second half, but not much. After another Mann field goal, quarterback Fran Tarkenton hit Sammy White with an eight-yard scoring pass to cut the deficit to 19-7. But two Oakland interceptions iced the victory. One set up Banaszak's two-yard TD run and cornerback Willie Brown returned another 75 yards for a score.

Coach John Madden watched his Raiders amass a Super Bowl-record 429 yards and Clarence Davis rush for 137. Fred Biletnikoff earned MVP honors with four receptions for 79 yards.

★★★★★★

 Pulling 'em in: Watched by a record crowd, Oakland won its first Super Bowl, handing Minnesota its fourth defeat, thanks to Fred Biletnikoff's four receptions.

SUPER BOWL XII

TM/©1977 NFL

JAN 15, 1978, AT LOUISIANA SUPERDOME, NEW ORLEANS

COWBOYS 27, BRONCOS 10

★★★★★★★★★★★★★★★★

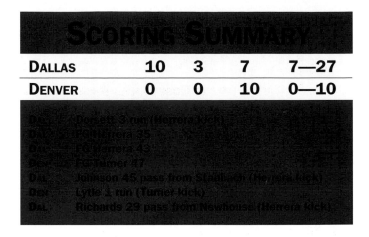

SCORING SUMMARY				
DALLAS	10	3	7	7—27
DENVER	0	0	10	0—10

Dal	Dorsett 3 run (Herrera kick)
Dal	FG Herrera 35
Dal	FG Herrera 43
Den	FG Turner 47
Dal	Johnson 45 pass from Staubach (Herrera kick)
Den	Lytle 1 run (Turner kick)
Dal	Richards 29 pass from Newhouse (Herrera kick)

Denver quarterback Craig Morton knew it wasn't going to be easy. But he never dreamed it would be so bad. Harried, battered and abused by his former teammates, Morton completed only 4 of 15 passes, threw four interceptions and watched the final 20 minutes from the sideline as good friend Roger Staubach directed the Cowboys to victory in the first indoor Super Bowl game.

The 75,583 fans who packed the New Orleans Superdome watched the Cowboys ride their defensive horses. Not only did the Dallas defense throttle Morton, it held the Broncos to 156 total yards, forced eight total turnovers, including four fumbles, and set up ten points. Defensive end Harvey Martin and tackle Randy White were so dominating they were named co-MVPs.

The Cowboys converted two of their interceptions into first-quarter points—Tony Dorsett's three-yard touchdown run and Efren Herrera's 35-yard field goal. Herrera connected from 43 yards in the second period to give the Cowboys a 13-0 halftime advantage that could have been a lot higher considering the Broncos had turned the ball over seven times and managed two first downs.

Morton made Dallas fans a little nervous when he drove the Broncos to a 47-yard Jim Turner field goal after the second-half kickoff. But Staubach answered with a 45-yard TD pass to Butch Johnson.

When a one-yard Rob Lytle run cut the deficit back to ten (20-10) late in the third quarter, Dallas administered the coup de grace—Robert Newhouse's 29 yard touchdown bomb to Golden Richards on a halfback pass.

 Dallas double-dip: Two defensive linemen, end Harvey Martin (79) and tackle Randy White (54), shared the MVP award after the Cowboys defeated Denver 27-10.

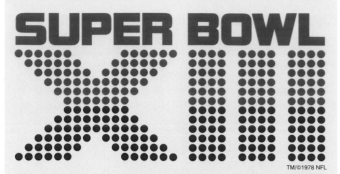

SUPER BOWL XIII

TM/©1978 NFL

JAN 21, 1979, AT THE ORANGE BOWL, MIAMI

STEELERS 35, COWBOYS 31

SCORING SUMMARY

PITTSBURGH	7	14	0	14—35
DALLAS	7	7	3	14—31

PIT	Stallworth 28 pass from Bradshaw (Gerela kick)
DAL	Hill 39 pass from Staubach (Septien kick)
DAL	Hegman 37 fumble recovery return (Septien kick)
PIT	Stallworth 75 pass from Bradshaw (Gerela kick)
PIT	Bleier 7 pass from Bradshaw (Gerela kick)
DAL	FG Septien 27
PIT	Harris 22 run (Gerela kick)
PIT	Swann 18 pass from Bradshaw (Gerela kick)
DAL	DuPree 7 pass from Staubach (Septien kick)
DAL	B Johnson 4 pass from Staubach (Septien kick)

The bruising "Steel Curtain" defense received most of the credit for Pittsburgh's first two Super Bowl triumphs, but victory No 3 belonged to the offense. Specifically to quarterback Terry Bradshaw, who threw for 318 yards and a record four touchdowns while earning MVP honors.

Bradshaw mesmerized a packed house at Miami's Orange Bowl with three touchdown strikes in a wild first half that produced a 21-14 Pittsburgh lead. Two of those strikes were to John Stallworth—a 28-yarder that gave the Steelers a 7-0 lead and a 75-yard bomb that tied the game at 14. The third, a seven-yarder to Rocky Bleier, gave Pittsburgh a lead it never relinquished.

The Cowboys, who had taken their 14-7 lead on Roger Staubach's 39-yard pass to Tony Hill and linebacker Mike Hegman's 37-yard romp with a fumble recovery, closed to within 21-17 on Rafael Septien's 27-yard third-quarter field goal. But the Steelers blew the game open with two touchdowns in a 19-second span of the fourth quarter.

Franco Harris's 22-yard run accounted for one and Bradshaw's 18-yard strike to Lynn Swann produced the other after a Dallas fumble. With 6:51 remaining, the Steelers were in control, 35-17. Or so everybody thought.

The ever-dangerous Staubach connected on a seven-yard TD strike to Billy Joe DuPree with 2:27 remaining and passed four yards to Butch Johnson for another score with 22 seconds left after the Cowboys recovered an onside kick. The victory wasn't sealed until another onside kick failed after the final touchdown.

 Going all the way: Pittsburgh wide receiver John Stallworth (82) made this 75-yard touchdown reception from Terry Bradshaw in the Steelers' 35-31 victory over Dallas.

JAN 20, 1980, AT THE ROSE BOWL, PASADENA, CAL

STEELERS 31, RAMS 19

A funny thing happened to the Steelers on their way to the coronation: they almost got crowned. Pittsburgh, seeking to become the first four-time Super Bowl winner and stake its claim as the greatest team of all time, needed a 73-yard fourth-quarter touchdown pass from Terry Bradshaw to dispatch a Rams team that had finished 9-7 during the regular season.

The Rams, who had been listed as 11-point underdogs, made Pittsburgh's run to immortality a difficult one. Moving the ball consistently against the "Steel Curtain" defense, the Rams surprisingly forged a 13-10 halftime lead on Cullen Bryant's one-yard run and two Frank Corral field goals. When the Steelers grabbed a 17-13 third-quarter lead on Bradshaw's 47-yard touchdown pass to Lynn Swann, everybody expected the Rams to do a quick fade. What they did was score quickly.

It took quarterback Vince Ferragamo only four plays to move the Rams 77 yards and reclaim the lead. Fifty of those yards came on a pass to Billy Waddy. The final 24 came on running back Lawrence McCutcheon's pass to Ron Smith.

With the Steelers trailing 19-17, Bradshaw decided it was time to think big. With less than 13 minutes remaining and buried on the Pittsburgh 27-yard line, Bradshaw sent Stallworth deep, hit him in stride at the Rams 34 and watched him race untouched toward the end zone for a 24-19 lead. Back in control, Bradshaw later connected with Stallworth on the same play for a 45-yard gain that set up a clinching touchdown—Franco Harris' one-yard run.

Unfazed by the closeness of their fourth Super Bowl victory in six years, the Steelers tried to answer the question on everybody's mind.

SCORING SUMMARY

LOS ANGELES	7	6	6	0	19
PITTSBURGH	3	7	7	14	31

PIT	FG Bahr 41
LA	Bryant 1 run (Corral kick)
PIT	Harris 1 run (Bahr kick)
LA	FG Corral 31
LA	FG Corral 45
PIT	Swann 47 pass from Bradshaw (Bahr kick)
LA	Smith 24 pass from McCutcheon (kick failed)
PIT	Stallworth 73 pass from Bradshaw (Bahr kick)
PIT	Harris 1 run (Bahr kick)

Bradshaw's best again: Pittsburgh quarterback Terry Bradshaw collected his second straight Super Bowl MVP award after the Steelers' fourth triumph, 31-19 over the Rams.

"Winning a fourth Super Bowl should put us in a special category," said cornerback Mel Blount. "I think this is the best team ever assembled. They talk about Vince Lombardi and the Packers, but I think the Chuck Noll era is even greater."

Despite throwing three interceptions, Bradshaw earned his second consecutive MVP award.

SUPER BOWL XV

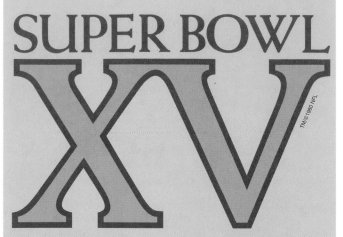

TM/© 1980 NFL

JAN 25, 1981, AT LOUISIANA SUPERDOME, NEW ORLEANS
RAIDERS 27, EAGLES 10

★★★★★★★★★★★★★★★★★

Quarterback Jim Plunkett completed his Cinderella season with a three-touchdown performance against the Eagles and the Raiders completed their Cinderella playoff run by becoming the first wild-card team to win a Super Bowl.

The veteran Plunkett, who had been buried on the Oakland bench for more than two years, took over for injured starter Dan Pastorini in Game 5 of the 1980 regular season. The reborn former Heisman Trophy winner led the Raiders to nine victories in his 11 starts and a wild-card playoff berth, a death sentence for all but one previous Super Bowl hopeful (the 1975 Cowboys, who lost in Super Bowl X).

SCORING SUMMARY

OAKLAND	14	0	10	3—27
PHILADELPHIA	0	3	0	7—10

But the Raiders swept through three playoff games and made their victory over the Eagles look easy. Plunkett threw a pair of touchdown passes to Cliff Branch (2 and 29 yards) and connected with running back Kenny King on an 80-yard bomb that broke the Eagles' back.

On the final play from scrimmage of the opening quarter with the Raiders already leading 7-0, a scrambling Plunkett fired to King on the left sideline, just over the outstretched arm of Eagles cornerback Herman Edwards, and King ran untouched for the longest touchdown play in Super Bowl history.

Leading 14-3 at halftime, the Raiders struck for ten third-quarter points to seal the victory. Plunkett, who completed 13 of 21 passes for 261 yards, earned MVP honors, but Raiders linebacker Rod Martin made a major contribution by intercepting a Super Bowl-record three Ron Jaworski passes.

Dick Vermeil's Eagles scored on Jaworski's eight-yard pass to Keith Krepfle and Tony Franklin's 30-yard field goal.

Wild at heart: Jim Plunkett's (16) two first-quarter touchdown passes helped the Oakland Raiders become the first wild card team to win the Super Bowl.

SUPER BOWL XVI

TM/©1981 NFL

JAN 24, 1982, AT PONTIAC SILVERDOME, PONTIAC, MICH
49ERS 26, BENGALS 21

★★★★★★★★★★★★★★★★

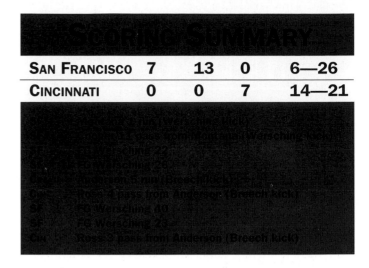

SCORING SUMMARY

SAN FRANCISCO	7	13	0	6—26
CINCINNATI	0	0	7	14—21

SF — Montana 1 run (Wersching kick)
SF — Cooper 11 pass from Montana (Wersching kick)
SF — FG Wersching 22
SF — FG Wersching 26
Cin — Anderson 5 run (Breech kick)
Cin — Ross 4 pass from Anderson (Breech kick)
SF — FG Wersching 40
SF — FG Wersching 23
Cin — Ross 3 pass from Anderson (Breech kick)

When the 49ers squared off against the Bengals in a battle of first-time Super Bowl participants, nobody knew what to expect. And that's exactly what 81,270 fans at the Pontiac Silverdome got—the unexpected.

Such as San Francisco's Super Bowl-record 92-yard drive that produced a second-quarter touchdown; Ray Wersching's record-tying four field goals; the 49ers' record 20-0 halftime lead, courtesy of three point-producing Cincinnati turnovers; a valiant Bengals comeback that fell just short, and a game-saving goal-line stand by the 49ers.

Coach Bill Walsh's 49ers appeared headed for an easy day when quarterback Joe Montana, the game's MVP, scored on a one-yard run and fired an 11-yard scoring pass to Earl Cooper, culminating the 92-yard drive. But the biggest blows were delivered when Wersching kicked two field goals in the final 18 seconds of the first half, the second after a fumbled kickoff.

The Bengals were down, but not out. Cincinnati quarterback Ken Anderson, who would set a Super Bowl record for completions

(25), scored on a five-yard third-quarter run and then directed the Bengals to a first-and-goal at the San Francisco 3. Fullback Pete Johnson reached the one on first down, but the Bengals failed on three tries from there. Johnson was stopped on a fourth-down plunge.

Having missed on that opportunity, Anderson threw a four-yard fourth-quarter touchdown pass to Dan Ross, cutting the deficit to 20-14. But two fourth-quarter Wersching field goals stretched the 49ers' advantage to 26-14, and another Anderson-to-Ross TD pass with 16 seconds remaining was too little, too late.

🏈 **Ray of light:** San Francisco was never headed in Super Bowl XVI, and kicker Ray Wersching's four field goals were a record for the game.

A SUPER LEAP FOR THE 49ERS

Time was running out for the 49ers in their bid to reach the team's first Super Bowl. Only 4:54 remained in their 1981 NFC Championship Game battle with Dallas and they were 89 yards away from a potential winning touchdown.

If a situation ever was made for Joe Montana, this was it. With his team trailing 27-21, the San Francisco quarterback began a march that would end with one of the most exciting plays in football history.

Mixing runs and passes and masterfully working the clock, Montana took the 49ers deep into Cowboys territory, finally setting up on third-and-three at the Dallas 6-yard line. Only a minute remained.

Montana, who had thrown earlier touchdown passes to Freddie Solomon and Dwight Clark, took the snap, rolled right and felt the pressure of three Dallas defenders. As he neared the sideline, he fired a high pass that appeared to be out of everybody's reach. But the 6-foot-4 Clark, stationed in the back of the end zone, jumped high and snared the ball with a fingertip catch. Ray Wersching's extra point made it final: 49ers 28, Cowboys 27. The victory sent the 49ers to their first Super Bowl. The Cowboys had set up Montana's heroics when Danny White fired a 21-yard fourth-quarter TD pass to Doug Cosbie for the 27-21 lead.

XVII SUPER BOWL

JAN 30, 1983, AT THE ROSE BOWL, PASADENA, CAL
REDSKINS 27, DOLPHINS 17

★★★★★★★★★★★★★★

It was the "Hogs" versus the "Killer Bees," Washington's huge offensive line versus Miami's swarming defense. In the end, size and strength won out. The unmentioned factors in that equation were bulldozing Redskins running back John Riggins and a Washington defense that did a little swarming of its own. Riggins earned MVP honors by rushing for a Super Bowl-record 166 yards, 43 coming on a fourth-and-one final-quarter touchdown romp that decided the game.

Miami's 17-13 fourth-quarter advantage was forged in a big-play first half that featured a 76-yard touchdown pass from David Woodley to Jimmy Cefalo and an electrifying 98-yard kickoff return by Fulton Walker after Washington had tied the game at ten. Walker's TD was the first on a kick return in Super Bowl history.

But the second half was all downhill for the Dolphins, who could penetrate the Washington defense for only 34 total yards. Neither Woodley nor backup quarterback Don Strock completed a second-half pass. It was just a matter of time.

The Redskins sliced their 17-10 halftime deficit to four on Mark Moseley's third-quarter field goal and took control in the final period when Riggins bolted off tackle for his dramatic game-winner. Quarterback Joe Theismann completed the scoring with his second TD pass, a six-yarder to Charlie Brown.

The championship was the first for a Washington team since 1942.

★★★★★★★

SCORING SUMMARY

	1	2	3	4	Total
MIAMI	7	10	0	0	—17
WASHINGTON	0	10	3	14	—27

MIA	Cefalo 76 pass from Woodley (von Schamann kick)
WAS	FG Moseley 31
MIA	FG von Schamann 20
WAS	Garrett 4 pass from Theismann (Moseley kick)
MIA	Walker 98 kickoff return (von Schamann kick)
WAS	FG Moseley 20
WAS	Riggins 43 run (Moseley kick)
WAS	Brown 6 pass from Theismann (Moseley kick)

★★★★★★

Unstoppable force: John Riggins' (44) 43-yard touchdown run put the Washington Redskins ahead to stay in their 27-17 Super Bowl XVII win over Miami.

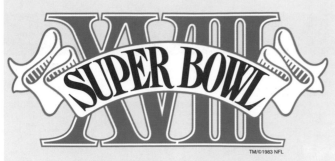

SUPER BOWL XVIII

JAN 22, 1984, AT TAMPA STADIUM

RAIDERS 38, REDSKINS 9

★★★★★★★★★★★★★★★★

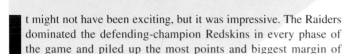

SCORING SUMMARY

WASHINGTON	0	3	6	0—9
LA RAIDERS	7	14	14	3—38

RAI	Jensen recovered blocked punt in end zone (Bahr kick)
RAI	Branch 12 pass from Plunkett (Bahr kick)
WAS	FG Moseley 24
RAI	Squirek 5 interception return (Bahr kick)
WAS	Riggins 1 run (kick blocked)
RAI	Allen 5 run (Bahr kick)
RAI	Allen 74 run (Bahr kick)
RAI	FG Bahr 21

It might not have been exciting, but it was impressive. The Raiders dominated the defending-champion Redskins in every phase of the game and piled up the most points and biggest margin of victory so far in Super Bowl history.

The first half belonged to the Los Angeles defense, which shut down the Redskins' powerful running attack, pressured quarterback Joe Theismann and produced a pair of touchdowns.

The first came when Derrick Jensen broke through the Washington line, blocked a Jeff Hayes punt and fell on the ball in the end zone. The second was a back-breaker. Seven seconds before halftime, linebacker Jack Squirek intercepted a Joe Theismann pass and returned it five yards for a score. Those big plays, sandwiched around Jim Plunkett's 12-yard scoring pass to Cliff Branch, gave the Raiders a 21-3 halftime lead.

The second half belonged to Raiders running back Marcus Allen, who scored a pair of touchdowns, earned MVP honors and easily outdistanced Washington running back John Riggins in their head-to-head duel. Allen finished with a Super Bowl-record 191 rushing yards, including a creative 74-yard third-quarter touchdown jaunt that iced the Raiders' victory. Ironically, he broke the rushing mark set a year earlier by Riggins (166).

Not only did the Raiders hold Riggins to 64 yards, his first sub-100-yard performance in seven postseason games, they also shut down a Redskins team that had won 11 consecutive games and outscored opponents by more than 250 points.

The Super Bowl victory was the third for the Raiders, their first since moving from Oakland to Los Angeles.

Into the hole: Los Angeles Raiders running back Marcus Allen bursts into the Washington defense with a Super Bowl XVIII MVP performance at Tampa Stadium.

SUPER XIX BOWL

TM/©1984 NFL

JAN 20, 1985, AT STANFORD STADIUM, STANFORD, CAL

49ERS 38, DOLPHINS 16

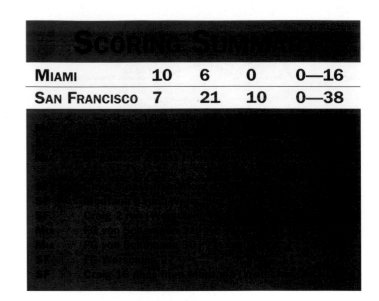

It was becoming increasingly clear this was no ordinary Joe. And when the dust had cleared on the 19th Super Bowl, Joe Montana had entrenched his name among the great big-game quarterbacks of football history.

Montana, who had won MVP honors in Super Bowl XVI, was nothing short of amazing in this one-sided duel with Dolphins quarterback Dan Marino. Montana completed 24 of 35 passes for a Super Bowl-record 331 yards and three touchdowns. He also scored on a six-yard run, scrambled for 59 yards and directed a diversified San Francisco offense that compiled a record 537 total yards.

It appeared early that Montana and the 49ers would be in for a real shootout. Marino quickly drove the Dolphins to a Uwe von Schamann field goal and answered Montana's 33-yard TD pass to Carl Monroe with a six-play drive that ended with a two-yard scoring pass to Dan Johnson for a 10-7 Miami lead.

But while the 49ers continued to move relentlessly up and down the field, San Francisco defensive coordinator George Seifert made adjustments that slowed Marino to a crawl. The Dolphins would manage only two field goals, one set up by a fumble, the rest of the way.

But Montana was not a one-man show. He received excellent support from Roger Craig (three touchdowns), Wendell Tyler and Dwight Clark, while Marino was forced to operate as a one-man offense. He completed 29 of 50 passes for 318 yards, but he also was sacked four times and harassed unmercifully.

 Glory grab: Roger Craig, making an acrobatic catch of this Joe Montana pass, became the first man to score three touchdowns in one Super Bowl.

JAN 26, 1986, AT LOUISIANA SUPERDOME, NEW ORLEANS

BEARS 46, PATRIOTS 10

SCORING SUMMARY

CHICAGO	13	10	21	2—46	
NEW ENGLAND	3	0	0	7—10	

NE	FG Franklin 36
CHI	FG Butler 28
CHI	FG Butler 24
CHI	Suhey 11 run (Butler kick)
CHI	McMahon 2 run (Butler kick)
CHI	FG Butler 24
CHI	McMahon 1 run (Butler kick)
CHI	Phillips 28 interception return (Butler kick)
CHI	Perry 1 run (Butler kick)
NE	Fryar 8 pass from Grogan (Franklin kick)
CHI	Safety, Waechter tackled Grogan in end zone

The big, bad, bragging Bears of Mike Ditka, featuring one of the greatest defenses in NFL history, were way too much for the conservative and outmanned Patriots in the 20th Super Bowl. The problem for New England was very basic.

The Patriots were a running team and nobody had been able to run on the Bears all season. Chicago ranked first against the run and in total defense, third against the pass. The once-beaten Bears had allowed 118 total rushing yards and no points in their previous two playoff contests.

The game opened on a curious note. On the Bears' second play, Walter Payton fumbled and New England's Larry McGrew recovered on the Chicago 19. Three plays later, 1:19 into the game, Tony Franklin gave the Patriots a 3-0 lead with a 36-yard field goal.

That was New England's best moment. The Chicago defense dropped a blanket on the Pats and quarterback Jim McMahon began carving them up offensively. By the end of the first quarter, it was 13-3. By halftime, the Bears led 23-3. A three-touchdown third period, highlighted by cornerback Reggie Phillips' 28-yard interception return, stretched the lead out of sight.

When all was said and done, statistics told a grim story for New England fans. The Patriots had managed only 123 total yards, seven on the ground. The Bears' 46 points were the most in Super Bowl history, as was the 36-point margin of victory. Chicago ran up 408 yards against a respected New England defense.

Behind you: New England's Steve Grogan is about to be sacked by Bears' defensive end Richard Dent, MVP in Chicago's 46-10 Super Bowl XX rout.

Picking and Hoping

COLLEGE DRAFT HAS BECOME A NATIONAL PHENOMENON

The football draft, known officially as the NFL Annual Selection Meeting, is not a recent innovation. NFL teams have been drafting college players to replenish their rosters since 1936, using a system very similar to the one they use today.

But the draft as an event is a recent phenomenon—an extravagant media happening with trimmings and trappings befitting a gala Hollywood event. The action is slow, the results are indecisive and the drama is infrequent and overplayed, but nobody can deny the grip football's talent auction holds on the American psyche.

On a weekend afternoon in late April, millions of hard-core football fanatics position themselves for a bird's-eye view of the much-anticipated selection process. Fans gather in a New York City ballroom, to cheer and jeer live announcements of their teams' picks. The rest tune into ESPN, assured of getting all the news from New York as well as hours and hours of "expert" analysis, interviews with everybody from agents to players' parents and live camera shots from

teams' war rooms, where decisions are made and phoned to New York. The ultimate moments come during the much-anticipated first round when Commissioner Paul Tagliabue steps to the New York microphone and announces another selection.

Nothing is analyzed, predicted and more rigorously debated than the NFL draft. "Draftniks" come out of the woodwork after every Super Bowl to study team weaknesses, analyze film and sift through scouting reports on the top college players. Draft guides are published, mock drafts are conducted and predictions of first-round selections are offered amid rumors of draft-day trades and position-switching deals. It's a fan's attempt to act as coach, general manager and football expert for a day.

Beyond the hype and prediction mania, the draft really is an opportunity for teams to reload, rebuild and recover past glories. They spend hundreds of thousands of dollars scouting college players and looking for the next Dick Butkus. Sometimes they find someone

Center stage: The podium stands vacant, waiting for commissioner Paul Tagliabue to approach and announce another draft selection.

was moved from winter to spring, allowing more time for player evaluation. Drafts also have gotten shorter, from 30 rounds in the 1940s and 1950s, to 12 in the 1970s, and seven in 1995. For television, the event was switched first to a Sunday-Monday format, then in 1995 to a Saturday-Sunday format.

There's a lot more money at stake today, too. Whereas Berwanger might have commanded a $5,000 contract in 1936, today's first-round picks expect millions of dollars. Every player's attributes are broken down and analyzed, from vertical leaps and 40-yard times to attitude and desire. Teams, anxious to hedge their investment, conduct pre-draft workouts and interviews, with every coach and personnel director knowing that a first-round mistake could cost their teams millions of dollars as well as fans and victories. They also know that some of the best picks have been made in the later rounds, necessitating thorough preparation, not to mention perseverance.

It all adds up to a kind of drama nobody could have foreseen 40 years ago when drafts were reported with agate type in the back of sports sections. Today's drafts garner major headlines and with that hype comes pressure—to pick wisely or face the consequences. Two things are at stake: pride and the future of 30 franchises.

And everybody is watching.

Heavy hitter: The Bengals, enjoying the luxury of consecutive No 1 overall picks, grabbed Ohio State defensive lineman Dan Wilkinson in 1994.

close, more often they find something less. In the world of computers and scouting combines, the art of picking future stars remains an inexact science.

Fundamentally, the draft is no different than the selection process used in 1936 when NFL leaders adopted the suggestion of Philadelphia Owner Bert Bell for a talent-distribution system that would bring more parity to the game. Teams agreed to draft in inverse order of their previous season's standing and the Eagles kicked off the process by grabbing University of Chicago halfback Jay Berwanger with the first pick. Ironically, Berwanger, winner of college football's first Heisman Trophy, refused to sign, even after the Eagles traded his rights to the Chicago Bears.

There have been variations in draft procedures, but the basic format remains the same. From 1947-58, "bonus choices" were awarded with the winner of a lottery getting the first pick. That winner dropped out of the lottery with the process continuing each year until every team had made a "bonus choice." In 1976, the draft

First things first: No 1 overall picks, like 1995 Cincinnati running back Ki-Jana Carter, find the draft process richly rewarding.

Where the Legends Live Forever

★★★★★★★★★★★★★★★★★★★ **PRO FOOTBALL HALL OF FAME**

I t's like crossing a time line into a different world, an ancient era of helmetless players, unsophisticated equipment and evolving playing styles. Every visitor to the Pro Football Hall of Fame in Canton, Ohio, is greeted, fittingly, by a 7-foot bronze statue of Jim Thorpe, which guards the ramp leading to a rendezvous with yesteryear.

It's a journey that begins in 1892 with the first chronicled professional football game and ends more than a century later amid the glitz and glitter of Super Bowl XXIX. The trip covers five buildings and is enhanced by television monitors, tape recordings, slide machines and a new theater presentation that offers the sights and sounds of modern pro football.

Today's five-building, juiced-up Hall of Fame, which entertains hundreds of thousands of yearly visitors, is the offshoot of a two-building, no-frills Hall of Fame that opened its doors to the public as part of a September 7, 1963, dedication ceremony. One of those original buildings was topped by a 52-foot, football-shaped dome that remains today as the Hall's signature feature.

Enshrinement: A huge crowd listens to the annual enshrinement ceremony outside the Pro Football Hall of Fame in Canton, Ohio. An NFL preseason exhibition game concludes the festivities.

There never was much debate about the Hall's logical site after Canton city officials began lobbying for the honor in the early 1960s. Canton offered historical significance (it was the site where the National Football League was born in 1920), a rugged football tradition (the Canton Bulldogs won two of the first four NFL championships) and a central location that allowed access from many large U.S. cities.

The NFL designated Canton as the official Pro Football Hall of Fame site on April 27, 1961, and groundbreaking began 16 months later on a wooded parkland site donated by the city. When the Hall of Fame was dedicated in 1963, 17 charter members were enshrined and the occasion was punctuated by a Hall of Fame preseason game at Fawcett Stadium, which is located directly across the street from the Hall's main facility. That game, a 16-7 Pittsburgh victory over Cleveland, was the second in a series that continues today as part of every enshrinement weekend.

The Hall of Fame membership has grown from its original 17-man cast to 185, including the five-member class of 1996. The election procedure is different from that used by any other sport.

Greetings: A 7-foot bronze statue of former great Jim Thorpe welcomes tourists to the Hall of Fame museum.

Fans nominate players for induction by writing to the Pro Football Hall of Fame and election is determined by a National Board of Selectors made up of writers from each NFL city, five at-large voters and a representative of the Pro Football Writers Association of America. Players must be retired for five years before they can be considered, coaches can be considered the year after retirement and other contributors can be elected at any time. The committee meets every year on the day before the Super Bowl and nominees must receive 80 percent of their votes for election. Four to seven members are added each year.

Hall of Fame weekend has become a late-summer event, featuring fashion shows, a civic banquet honoring the enshrinees, a parade that draws 200,000-plus viewers, the enshrinement ceremonies and the AFC-NFC football game that features rotating teams and draws a 23,000-plus crowd. And, of course, there's the museum itself, which has entertained more than 5 million fans since 1963.

Among the highlights of the tour are an exhibition rotunda that recounts the game's history, an art gallery featuring award-winning football photographs, a research library, the twin enshrinement halls, a mementos room, the Super Bowl room and an area that electronically chronicles the evolution of the football-television relationship.

It's safe to say that the growth of the Hall of Fame has mirrored the growth of the sport it represents. When that 17-member charter class was inducted in 1963, the original two-building complex contained 19,000 square feet of interior display space. Three subsequent expansions have more than quadrupled that figure to 79,650 square feet.

The following biographies detail the careers of 50 of professional football's Hall of Fame players and founding fathers:

121, 125
Lamonica, Daryle 31, 77, 81
Landry, Tom 7, 17, 19, 39, 70, 121, 125
Lane, Dick 125
Langer, Jim 125
Langham, Antonio 20
Lanier, Willie 27, 125
Largent, Steve 34, 57, 60, 125
Lary, Yale 40, 125
Lavelli, Dante 13, 20, 125
Layden, Elmer 12
Layne, Bobby 13, 40, 121, 125
Le Clair, Jim 22
Leemans, Alphonse 125
Lett, Leon 103
Levy, Marv 21
Lillard, Joe 13
Lilly, Bob 39, 51, 70, 115, 122, 125
Lipps, Louis 109
Little, Larry 28, 125
Lloyd, Greg 32
Lofton, James 41
Lohmiller, Chip 101
Lombardi, Vince 7, 14, 15, 18, 41, 74-77, 89, 122, 125
Long, Howie 31
Lott, Ronnie 47, 58, 64
Luckman, Sid 11, 18, 38, 51, 122, 125
Lyman, Roy 125

M

Mackey, John 25, 80, 125
Madden, John 31, 68, 86
Malavasi, Ray 46
Manley, Dexter 49
Mann, Errol 86
Manning, Archie 115
Mara, Tim 10, 122, 125
Marchetti, Gino 25, 125
Marchibroda, Ted 20, 25
Marino, Dan 7, 17, 19, 28, 55, 59, 94, 115
Marlin, Tony 33
Marshal, Jim 42
Marshal, Leonard 44
Marshall, George Preston 10, 106, 122, 125
Martin, Curtis 29
Martin, Eric 43
Martin, George 44
Martin, Harvey 39, 70, 87
Martin, Rod 90
Mathis, Terance 36
Matson, Ollie 108, 125
Matte, Tom 25
Matuszak, John 31
Maynard, Don 30, 125
Maynes, Reuben 43
Maxie, Brett 37
McAfee, George 125
McClanahan, Brent 86
McClinton, Curtis 76
McConkey, Phil 96
McCormack, Mike 62, 125
McCutcheon, Lawrence 46, 89
McElhenny, Hugh 125
McGee, Max 41, 75, 76
McGrew, Larry 95
McMahon, Jim 38, 95
McMichael, Steve 38
McNair, Steve 24
McNair, Todd 24
McNeil, Freeman 30
McNeill, Fred 86
Means, Natrone 26
Mecklenburg, Karl 23
Mercer, Mike 76
Metcalf, Eric 36
Metcalf, Terry 35, 109
Miami Dolphins 16, 18, 28, 42, 49, 81-83, 92, 94
Michaels, Lon 78
Michalske, Mike 41, 125
Miller, Chris 36, 46
Millner, Wayne 125
Mills, Sam 37, 43
Minnesota Vikings 32, 42, 43, 54,

79, 83, 84, 86
Mirer, Rick 34
Mitchell, Bobby 125
Mitchell, Scott 40
Mitler, Red 23
Mix, Ron 15, 51, 125
Modell, Art 20
Monk, Art 49, 60, 109
Monroe, Carl 94
Montana, Joe 61, 7, 17, 27, 47, 64, 73, 75, 91, 94, 98, 99, 104, 109
Montgomery, Wilbert 45
Montoya, Max 22
Moon, Warren 26, 42
Moore, Derrick 37
Moore, Lenny 25, 122, 125
Mora, Jim 43
Morgan, Stanley 29
Morrall, Earl 78
Morris, Joe 44, 96
Morris, Mercury 16, 28, 51, 82
Morton, Craig 23, 80
Mosely, Mark 92
Motley, Marion 13, 20, 51, 122, 125
Muncie, Chuck 33, 109
Muñoz, Anthony 22, 58, 62
Murchison, Clint Jnr 39
Murray, Eddie 103, 109
Musso, George 11, 38, 125
Myhra, Steve 7, 14,

N

Nagurski, Bronco 9, 11, 38, 50, 122, 125
Namath, Joe 15, 17, 25, 30, 51, 54, 74-75, 78, 122, 125
Nattiel, Ricky 87
Neale, Earl 125
Nevers, Eric 9
Nevers, Ernie 35, 50, 122, 125
New England Patriots 16, 29, 38, 55, 63, 95
New Orleans Saints 43, 48
New York Giants 8, 11, 13, 29, 44, 54, 67, 68, 96, 100
New York Jets 15, 16, 25, 30, 78
Newhouse, Robert 39, 87
Nitschke, Ray 41, 50, 122, 125
Noll, Chuck 7, 16, 18, 32, 84, 89, 101, 125
Nomellini, Leo 115, 125
Norton, Ken 102
Norwood, Scott 100
Novacek, Jay 39, 102
Nowatzke, Tom 80

O

Oakland Raiders 17, 31, 34, 93
O'Brien, Jim 80
O'Brien, Ken 30, 55, 59, 109, 115
O'Donnell Neil 30, 32
Oakland Raiders 17, 23, 31, 33, 42, 45, 77, 81, 86, 90
Okoye, Christian 27
Olsen, Merlin 122, 125
Osborn, Dave 79, 84, 108
Osborne, Jim 66
Otis, Jim 35
Otto, Jim 15, 125
Owen, Steve 125

P

Page, Alan 42, 125
Parcells, Bill 19, 29, 44, 58
Pardee, Jack 26
Paris, Bubba 98
Parker, Clarence 125
Parker, Jim 125
Parmalee, Bernie 28
Parmer, Jim 66
Pastorini, Dan 26, 115
Patera, Jack 34
Payton, Walter 63, 7, 17, 38, 50, 51, 53, 64, 65, 95, 125
Pearson, Drew 39, 85
Pegram, Erric 36

Periman, Brett 40
Perry William 38
Perry, Joe 125
Pete, Rodney 40
Petitbon, Richie 49
Philadelphia Eagles 10, 11, 13, 45, 71, 90
Phillips, Bum 26, 43
Phillips, Reggie 95
Phillips, Wade 23
Phoenix Cardinals 17
Pickens, Carl 22
Pihos, Pete 125
Pitts, Elijah 76
Pittsburgh Pirates 10
Pittsburgh Steelers 16, 22, 32, 42, 58, 81 84-85, 88-89
Plom, Milt 20
Plunkett, Jim 31, 58, 90, 115
Policy, Carmen 73
Pollard, Fritz 13
Portsmouth Spartans 10, 40
Pruitt, Greg 20
Pruitt, Mike 20

R

Rashad, Ahmad 42
Ray, Hugh 125
Rechichar, Bert 108
Reed, Andre 21
Reed, Jake 42
Reeves, Dan 12, 23, 44, 46, 54, 54, 125
Reich, Frank 37
Renfro, Mel 108
Reynolds, Hacksaw 47
Rhein, Joe 105
Rhett, Errict 7, 48
Rhodes, Ray 45
Rice, Jerry 64, 7, 47, 60, 73, 75, 98, 99, 104
Richards, Golden 39, 87
Riggins, John 49, 51, 75, 92, 93, 125
Riggs, Gerald 36, 101
Riley, Pat 115
Ringo, Jim 41, 56, 125
Rison, Andre 20, 36
Roberts, Ray 34
Robeson, Paul 13
Robinson, Dave 41
Robinson, Eddie 26
Robinson, John 46, 53
Robinson, Johnny 15
Robustelli, Andy 125
Rooney, Art 10, 32, 122, 125
Rosenbloom, Carroll 46
Ross, Bobby 33
Ross, Dan 91
Rossi, Cal 114
Rozelle, Pete 7, 14, 15, 17, 123, 125
Ruth, Babe 8
Ryan, Buddy 35, 45, 55
Ryan, Frank 20
Rypien, Mark 49, 60, 101

S

Saban, Lou 21
Salaam, Rashaan 38
San Diego Chargers 32, 33, 47, 64, 72-73, 104
San Francisco 49ers 12, 13 18, 21, 29, 33, 39, 47, 58, 62, 73, 91, 94, 98-99, 104
Sanders, Barry 65, 7, 18, 40, 67
Sanders, Chris 24
Sanders, Deion 36
Sanders, Ricky 49, 97
Saver, George 30
Sayers, Gale 38, 53, 109, 115, 123, 125
Schmidt, Joe 40, 125
Schottenheimer, Marty 20, 27
Schramm, Tex 125
Schwartz, Bryan 26
Scott, Jake 28, 82
Searce, Jackie Leon 26
Seattle Seahawks 17, 24, 34,

56, 69
Seau, Junior 7, 33
Seifert, George 17, 18, 47, 94, 99
Selmon, Lee Roy 48, 115, 125
Settle, John 36
Shanahan, Mike 23, 31
Sharpe, Sterling 60
Shula, David 22
Shula, Don 7, 16, 17, 18, 22, 28, 59, 82, 83
Shuler, Heath 49
Simmons, Clyde45
Simms, Phil 44, 96, 109
Simpson, OJ 16, 21, 51, 53, 58, 109, 123, 125
Sims, Billy 40
Sims, Keith 28
Singletary, Mike 66, 7, 38
Sipe, Brian 20
Slater, Duke 13
Smith, Bruce 21
Smith, Bubba, 25
Smith, Dennis 23
Smith, Don 100
Smith, Emmitt 67, 17, 39, 52, 75, 102, 103
Smith, Jackie 35, 125
Smith, Jimmy 97
Smith, Neil 27
Smith, Timmy 75
Snell, Andre 21
Snell, Matt 78
Solomon, Freddie 47
Speedie, Mac 13, 20
Spielman, Chris 65
St. Clare, Bob 125
St. Louis Cardinals 14, 17, 35
St. Louis Rams 46
Stabler, Ken 31, 81, 86
Stalls, Dave 70
Stallworth, John 75, 88
Starr, Bart 7, 14, 18, 41, 50, 75, 76, 77, 115, 122, 125
Staubach, Roger 7, 17, 39, 51, 81, 84, 85, 87, 88, 109, 123, 125
Stautner, Ernie 125
Steagles, The 12
Stenerud, Jan 79, 125
Stepnoski, Mark 26
Stewart, James 26
Still, Art 109
Stram, Hank 27
Strock, Don 92
Strode, Woody 13
Strong, Ken 125
Stydahar, Joe 38, 115, 125
Swan, Lynn 50, 65, 88, 89
Swilling, Pat 43
Switzer, Barry 39

T

Tagliabue, Paul 112
Talley, Darryl 21
Tampa Bay Buccaneers 17, 34, 48
Tarkenton, Fran 42, 51, 55, 83, 84, 86, 108, 123, 125
Tatum, Jack 31
Taylor, Charley 49, 64, 108, 125
Taylor, Jim 41, 51, 76, 125
Taylor, John 47, 61, 73
Taylor, Lawrence 68, 7, 44, 69, 96
Taylor, Otis 79
Testaverde, Vinny 20
Theismann, Joe 49, 92, 93
Theismann, Joe 109
Thigpen, Yancy 32
Thomas, Derrek 69, 27
Thomas, Duane 39, 80, 81
Thomas, Rodney 24
Thomas, Thurman 21, 100, 101-103
Thompson, Tommy 45
Thorpe, Jim 8, 118, 123, 125
Tittle, YA 44, 123, 125
Tobin, Bill 63
Tobin, Vince 35
Todd, Richard 30
Tolliver, Billy Joe 69
Toon, Al 30
Townsend, Greg 62

Trafton, George 38, 125
Trippi, Charley 35, 51, 125
Trudeau, Jack 37
Tunnell, Emlen 125
Turner, Clyde 125
Turner, Eric 20
Turner, Jim 78
Turner, Norv 49
Tyler, Wendell 94

U

Unitas, Johnny 7, 13, 14, 25, 51, 78, 80, 108, 115, 123, 125
Upshaw, Gene 125

V

Van Brocklin, Norm 13, 36, 46, 125
Van Buren, Steve 13, 45, 51, 123, 125
Van Eeghen, Mark 31
Vermeil, Dick 45, 68, 90
Volk, Rich 80
Von Schamann, Uwe 94

W

Waddy, Billy 89
Walden, Bobby 84
Walker, Doak 40, 125
Walker, Fulton 92
Walker, Wesley 30
Walsh, Bill 7, 17, 47, 61, 64, 91, 98, 99, 101, 125
Wannstedt, Dave 38
Ware, Andre 40
Warfield, Paul 28, 51, 64, 108, 123, 125
Warner, Curt 34
Warren, Chris 34, 109
Washington Redskins 11, 16, 40, 49, 60, 82, 92, 93, 97, 101
Washington, James 102, 103
Washington, Kenny 13
Washington, Mike 48
Waterfield, Bob 12, 13, 46, 51, 123, 125
Waters, Charlie 39, 70
Watters, Rickey 45, 47, 104
Webb, Richmond 28
Webster, Alex
Weinmeister, Arnie 125
Werblin, Sonny 15
Wersching, Ray 91
White, Byron (Whizzer) 11, 69, 71
White, Danny 91
White, Dwight 51, 84
White, Randy 39, 56, 70, 87, 125
White, Reggie 71, 7, 41, 45
Wilder, James 48
Wilkinson, Dan 22
Williams, Doug 48, 49, 75, 97
Williams, Harvey 31
Williams, Reggie 22
Willis, Bill 13, 20, 125
Wilson, George 28
Wilson, Larry 125
Winder, Sammy 23
Winslow, Kellen 17, 33, 72, 125
Wood, Barry 27
Wood, Richard 48
Wood, Willie 41, 125
Woodly, David 28, 92
Woods, Ickey 22
Woodson, Rod 32
Wright, Eric 47
Wyche, Sam 48

Y

Yepremian, Garo 82, 83, 109
Young, Steve 73, 7, 17, 47, 64, 75, 104

Z

Zorn, Jim 34